Playwriting

What makes a story work on stage? This book offers a practical guide for all those who are involved in the creation of text for live performance. Containing a wealth of exercises, *Playwriting* takes the reader through each stage of the process of making a play, and includes chapters on:

- Working on themes and issues
- Building a character
- Finding the story
- Writing a second draft.

These practical exercises can be used in a wide range of contexts: as a step-by-step guide for the individual playwright, as a handy resource for a teacher or workshop leader, or as a stimulus for a group-devised play. All the exercises can be adapted for the specific context. This is the ideal handbook for anyone who engages with playwriting and who is concerned with bringing a story to life on the stage.

Noël Greig has spent the last thirty years working as an actor, director and playwright. He has taught courses in playwriting, acting and theatre history and is currently involved in making theatre with and for young people, working with youth groups around the world, and encouraging new writing.

'Noël Greig is a gifted playwright and teacher. His ability to come up with a range of processes, each distinct and unique to the needs of any given group, is extraordinary. I have witnessed wonderful writing emerge from groups who have never considered themselves as writers, and emerging and established playwrights seeking him out as dramaturge and mentor.'

Kully Thiarai, Artistic Director,
Leicester Haymarket Theatre

'I have spent half my career waiting for this book to be written. Noël Greig is the original great communicator, playwright, mentor, tutor, support, coach and inspiration. His knowledge and ability should be listed as a national asset. Noël's mantra is "only connect" and I have yet to find an individual who has met him, and has failed to do this on a thousand and one levels. Buy this book and be prepared to be wowed.'

Ola Animashawun, Associate Director, Young Writers
Programme, The Royal Court Theatre, London

'There can be no better teacher or mentor than Noël Greig. If he can't teach you how to write a play, no-one can.'

Haresh Sharma, Resident Playwright,
The Necessary Stage, Singapore

'I have observed Noël Greig's dramaturgical processes open doors to thrilling creativity: from the fifteen-year old discovering the joys of play-writing, to the mature playwright breaking through to new possibilities. I have witnessed children and adults alike moved to compassionate insights about humanity through the power of his plays. A master at facilitating new voices and expressing the complexities of our age, at the core of every aspect of Noël's work is always rigour, grace and sensitivity.'

Rosamunde Hutt, Director,
Theatre Centre, London

'I have worked with Noël Greig for over 20 years and continue to be inspired by his work with writers from all over the world and from many different backgrounds. His methods have had a tremendous impact on the writers themselves and they have influenced much of the work that we do here with emerging playwrights.'

Elyse Dodgson, Associate Director,
Head of International Department,
The Royal Court Theatre, London

'A terrific introduction to the creation of texts for live theatre . . . Greig not only describes exercises but provides a step-by-step process of play development for both individual writers and an astonishing range of groups who might devise work collaboratively. The book is also a lovely introduction to the appreciation of dramatic literature, as Greig demystifies how disparate well-known playwrights contend with the same issues as the novice writer. This is a book, like Viola Spolin and Augusto Boal's classic games' texts, that workshop facilitators should not be without!'

Jan Cohen-Cruz, New York University

Playwriting

A practical guide

Noël Greig

Routledge
Taylor & Francis Group

LONDON AND NEW YORK

First published 2005
by Routledge
2 Park Square, Milton Park, Abingdon, Oxon OX14 4RN

Simultaneously published in the USA and Canada
by Routlege
711 Third Avenue, New York, NY 10017

Routledge is an imprint of the Taylor & Francis Group, an informa business

© 2005 Noël Greig

Typeset in Janson and Univers by
Newgen Imaging Systems (P) Ltd, Chennai, India
Printed by the MPG Books Group in the UK

British Library Cataloguing in Publication Data
A catalogue record for this book is available from the British Library

Library of Congress Cataloging in Publication Data
Greig, Noël.
    Playwriting: a practical guide / Noël Greig.
        p. cm.
    1. Playwriting.   I. Title.

PN1661.G715 2004
808.2′2–dc22   2004007129

ISBN 13: 978–0–415–31044–4 (pbk)

For Trevor John, who taught me how to think
and
Vic Lee, who taught me the value of the word

Contents

Preface

To be part of an audience at a live drama is an opportunity to experience the critical or self-conscious dimension to our shared existence. Gathering together to witness a performance, we are celebrating our ability – our need – to reflect on the conditions that make (or unmake) us human. Private concerns are made public; the invisible is made visible. In the course of my working life as a theatre practitioner I have witnessed this deep-seated human need for the ritual that expresses our common humanity in a wide range of contexts. The group-devised play in a school hall, the large-cast community pageant-play, political street theatre in India, dance-and-song drama in Africa, location-specific work performed in libraries, car-parks, on beaches and in abandoned buildings, professional and amateur performance, major world drama, experimental work and new plays in small studios and on main stages; I make no distinction between them in terms of their function. The little scene written and performed in the classroom may pass off in an afternoon and never be heard of again. The new play written by one author and presented on the stage of a national theatre may pass into the canon of great, universal works. But as events that bring us together and connect us with each other they are equal.

Who the book is for

This book is intended for all individuals and groups who are engaged with 'the word' as part of the development of live performance. The practical work it offers has been developed through my engagement with a wide range of communities and contexts: educational- and youth-theatre, community groups (geographical- or interest-led), professional and amateur, within the UK and internationally. All of it can be applied to the type of text being developed for the particular context and, almost without exception, every exercise can be adapted to any context. An exercise that I have used with an individual writer in a South African township has worked equally well with a youth-theatre group in a UK city; one used in a primary school can similarly adapt to a class with students on an MA playwriting course. I will give some guidance on the adaptation of exercises in Appendix A.

How to use the book

The book is arranged into nine chapters. Chapter 1 offers a range of exercises that enable first-time writers to engage with basic elements of writing plays, or for groups to begin to create material collaboratively. Subsequent chapters look in detail at specific aspects of the craft: character-creation, play-structure, etc. Some of this work will have particular interest to the individual playwright or to creative-writing groups, but much of it also will be of use to the process of group-devising or collaboration. The final chapter gives some examples of models for large group-devised or collaboratively written plays. Notes for facilitators and group leaders are included in Appendix B.

Each exercise is presented in a step-by-step manner, with examples and outcomes. I have indicated – where appropriate – an approximate time frame for exercises. I have also indicated those exercises that can be undertaken by an individual, as well as in a group. A few exercises (15, 16, 17, 19, and 90) I have to date used only with primary class children; but I would not wish this to mean that they might not have a use in other contexts, nor that all the other work cannot be adapted to this age group.

You may use the book in a variety of ways:

- As a step-by-step guide to the construction of a whole narrative, both individually and group-written.
- As a 'dip-in' resource for one-off workshops and courses.
- As a source of models for large-scale performance projects.

Throughout the book I have referred to certain extant texts as examples of how particular exercises work. They tend to be proven and well-known works by such writers as Arthur Miller, Harold Pinter, William Shakespeare, etc. I have chosen them because I am very familiar with them – through having acted in or directed them – and because they should be readily available to any reader. They represent a rather narrow cultural frame but, in your application of the exercises, use works that you are familiar with and which may reflect a broader frame.

Exposure to the work of writers from different cultures has been central to my own development, and although Miller *et al.* may exemplify some of the underlying first-principles of the craft of the playwright, they are by no means the sole source of guidance, inspiration and consolation. When I saw the play *A Raisin in the Sun*, by the black American writer Lorraine Hansberry, it spoke to me as much about my own British family as it did about the fictional Ruth Younger and hers in Chicago. Great narratives speak to the world (and I include here the great fables, folk-tales and fairy-stories, many of which I regularly use and refer to in this book). I remember being in Canada, listening to Thomson Highway, a first-nation writer and a leading playwright there. He was talking about Jane Austen and the Bronte sisters, the influence they had had on his work and thinking, and how they belonged to him just as much as anyone. The black British playwright Kwame Kwei-Armah recently wrote:

> For me, the challenge is to make the stage a forum that allows universal themes to shine and refract through the humanity of my cultural lenses. That, I believe, does more than several hundred pieces of race-relations legislation. It makes us all part of the human family. Equally. That's political.
>
> (Kwame Kwei-Armah, *The Guardian*, September 2003)

A fifteen-year old schoolgirl, in a workshop I was leading, wrote this: 'In this universe, we all play a different tune on the same violin.' The black British philosopher C.L.R. James wrote this: 'Beethoven belongs as much to West Indians as he does to Germans, since his music is now part of the human heritage.'

It has been a great privilege to work with so many writers, from so many cultures and contexts. In this instant-electronic age, where we are told that the desire for reflectivity is on the wane, the fact that so many people – increasingly perhaps – wish to engage with their inner lives through creative writing is greatly encouraging. I hope that the contents of this book help to encourage that act of rebellion against the media sound-bite and political platitude.

Note: For the purposes of international distribution, the title of the book appears as 'Playwriting'. In the body of the text the author has used the form more familiar in the UK: 'playwrighting'.

Acknowledgements

Many of the exercises in this book have been developed during projects or workshops I have been leading with other theatre-arts practitioners: writers, actors, directors, designers and composers. All of us who work in the field inspire and borrow from each other, and I would like to thank the following friends and colleagues who have contributed to the development of my work as a teacher and tutor.

Ola Animashawun, Shabina Aslam, John Binnie, Becky Chapman, Maya Chowdry, Phil Clark, Therese Collins, Simon Deacon, Luke Dixon, Elyse Dodgeson, Lawrence Evans, Rosy Fordham, Rosamunde Hutt, Michael Judge, Libby Mason, Tony McBride, Mike McCormack, Carl Miller, Brenda Moor, Stuart Mullins, Philip Osment, Kate Owen, Mary Robson, Shabnam Shabnazi, Haresh Sharma, Kully Thiarai, Philip Tyler, Manjinder Virk, Michelene Wandor.

Extracts from *Final Cargo* by Noël Greig are used courtesy of Nelson Thornes. *Final Cargo* © Nelson Thornes 2004, originally published by Thomas Nelson (Walton-on-Thames), 1994 and edited by Andy Kempe.

1 Getting going and warming up

Actors begin rehearsals with a physical and vocal warm-up. This helps them to clear the body and the mind of daily distractions and tensions, focus them on the space they are in and prepare them for the task in hand. Writers also need strategies to clear themselves of the clutter and access the open channel between the mind, the hand and the sheet of paper (or the screen). This might include some sort of physical activity; a friend of mine, who writes at home but needs to separate her work from the washing-up, does the morning domestic routine, then goes out for a walk and eventually 'walks to work'. If I am working with a group, I will generally start with some sort of physical activity or game. Even then, the blank page (or screen) can still be sitting there, waiting for the words that refuse to come, and some form of kick-start writing activity can be useful. What follows are a range of exercises designed to stimulate the 'writing-muscle'. The first few are general 'warm-up' exercises. I will then move on to 'introductory' exercises for work that will be dealt with in greater detail in the following chapters. The chapter may be used in a range of ways according to your needs, for example:

- As a template for an introductory course in playwrighting.
- As a menu from which to construct a one-off workshop.
- As a stimulus for a group-devising process.
- As a range of 'getting-going' exercises for when you have come back from your morning walk.

MEMORY

Writing is, as much as anything, an act of memory. Not necessarily as a recording of your own life and history, but rather as an attempt to capture in words impressions made on the senses by the world around us. What did that type of rain feel like? What was that woman's unusual way of expressing herself? What made the journey to work or school today different from any other of those journeys?

Exercise 1 Going for a walk

Participants: All groups, individual (10–30 minutes)

1 Go for a walk. Round the block, round the park, or if you are in a school, round the playground or the playing field. Be conscious of what are you seeing and hearing. Be aware of your body moving in space, the way you are breathing, the ground beneath your feet, and the air around you. What are you seeing, hearing and feeling? Hear the words in your head. Allow phrases to form themselves. Allow the rhythm of the walking to infect the rhythm of the words in your head. If you start to speak the words, let it happen.

2 Return from your walk.

3 Write:

   • Ten things you saw.
   • Five sounds you heard.
   • Three feelings you experienced.
   • One question that is prompted by what you saw, heard or felt.

Exercise 2 Lying on the floor

Participants: All groups, individual (5–10 minutes)

1 Lie on the floor in a comfortable position and close your eyes. Listen to the sounds outside the building or the room. After a minute or so, listen to the sounds inside the room. Finally, listen to the sounds inside your own body. Allow your hearing-sense to travel back-and-forth between these distances, identifying the specific sounds.

2 Write:

   • The type and quality of the sounds you heard.
   • One question about anything you heard or felt.

Exercise 3 Thinking about your life
Part one

Participants: All groups, individual (5–10 minutes)

1 Walk around the room (or if you are in a small space, sit somewhere comfortably). Allow yourself to feel relaxed and open. *Think about*

your life, the whole of it, as if it is a river running past you. Allow memories to flow past. Find something you remember that is of interest – an event, a moment, an image – and explore it. Then go and write it down, as one word, a few words or a sentence.

2   Start walking again (or sit back). Allow the river to flow again, letting the memory you have written slide away. *Think of your life last year*, as if it were a video. Find something of interest, something that was important or significant, and replay the scene over a few times. Summarise it in a few words or a line, then write it down.

3   *Think of your life this year* and repeat the process.

4   *Think of your life last week* and repeat the process.

5   Look at everything you have written, find three or four questions the words and phrases prompt, then write them down.

Part two – thinking about your life
Participants: All groups (10–20 minutes)

1   Begin with and complete Exercise 3 (part one).

2   Walk around the room again. Be aware of the other people in the space but work on your own.

3   Go and look at the first memory you wrote down. Close your eyes and say it to yourself. Walk around the room. Tell the memory to a chair, the window, the wall, or any other object in the room.

4   Find a partner. Listen to their memory. Repeat it and learn it. Tell your partner your memory, and they will repeat and learn it.

5   Swap memories. Forget your own memory, you have given it away. Walk around the room again, with your partner's memory. It is now yours.

6   Everyone collect together in the middle of the room, as close as possible, but without touching. Everyone has someone else's memory. Close your eyes. Tell to the group as much of the memory as you can. Don't rush, and avoid speaking over each other. Focus on everything that is said. Everyone will have heard all the memories now. You won't hold all of them in your mind, just fragments, images that have stayed with you.

7   Work on your own, writing down as much as you can remember from all that has been said – words, images, phrases, scraps of information. Use these notes to write a short piece beginning 'I remember...'. Include everything you have jotted down, re-arranging and adding other words where you need to.

8   Feed the individual work back to the group. What similar/different approaches have been adopted? What images stand out most?

Part three – thinking about your life
Participants: All groups (6–8 minutes for each stage)

1 Repeat Exercise 3 (part two), using the memory from last year, and the memory from this year, and the memory from last week. Each time, the process of listening, remembering and then writing the final piece should become more fluid.

2 Read out the results of the task. How have people used the same material differently? Were there images that came up a few times?

Exercise 4 Personal memory and shared memory
Participants: All groups (5–10 minutes)

You can adapt Exercise 3 (parts one, two and three) to any category of memory.

For example, find these three memories:

1 A very personal memory, one which no one else in the world could have.

2 A local memory, something shared by quite a lot of people in your community, street, school, etc., but not by the wider world.

3 A world memory, something shared by many people around the globe.

Outcome

These first exercises have enabled us to explore 'memory' and how it is recorded in writing. They have addressed a range of questions that are useful to us as writers: What is memory? How do we remember things? What do we remember and why? What is good memory, what is bad memory? What is true memory, what is false memory? What do I mean when I say, 'We are what we remember and how we remember it'?

INSTANT WRITING

At certain stages in the process, you do not need to plan. Indeed, 'planning ahead' can often be a block to the initial raw impulse. In schools, the fear of 'not getting it right' can inhibit the imagination; the following exercises (useful to all writers) can dispel this fear.

Exercise 5 Count and write

Participants: All groups, individual (2 minutes)

1 Count to 10 and write a description of how you look.
2 Count to 20 and write a description of today's weather.
3 Count to 50 and write a description of what you did yesterday.
4 Count to 100 and write a detailed description of the room you are in.

Exercise 6 Pink elephants

Participants: All groups, individual (3 minutes)

Think of pink elephants and write an account of what you did yesterday.

Exercise 7 I am writing

Participants: All groups, individual (3–5 minutes)

In Exercises 5 and 6 you were writing without thinking ahead. This time you will again be 'just writing', but there will be no numbers or pink elephants or given subjects.

1 You are going to write, but until you start you will have no idea what is going to come out.
2 Start with the words 'I am writing...' and do not stop.
3 If you find that, even if only for a second, your mind feels blank, just write 'I am writing, I am writing, I am writing...' until something else appears.
4 Don't plan, don't censor yourself, just write.
5 Ready, steady... go. (See Example 7.1.)
6 When you have finished, underline words, phrases and sentences that you particularly liked. (See Example 7.2.)

Example 7.1

Before starting work this morning – my first day on this book – I did this exercise myself. What came out was the following jumble, including the bad grammar and spelling:

> I am writing because I am starting to write this book what is a book a book is something between hard covers no not that it can be between

papercovers and its called a paperback my back is aching at the moment so I'm nt looking forward to sitting at the machine and typing in fact my back is so bad I think I'll have to lie down but I cant lie down because I have to carry on with this exercise for the book the book the book I cant think of oh yes I can... etc.

Example 7.2

From my own effort I liked the rhythm of 'papercovers and its called a paperback my back'.

Outcome

Even at this very simple stage of the process, we can learn to value quirkiness and originality in what we write, and to trust our instincts.

Exercise 8 Music and words

Participants: All groups, individual

Music and rhythm can provide an excellent stimulus to the writing process.

1   Close your eyes and listen to a piece of music for a few moments.
2   Let the music continue. Write a speech on a particular subject: war, peace, love, football, etc. Don't plan ahead. Allow the music to filter into what you are writing, the words you use, etc.

Exercise 9 Instant book

Participants: All groups, individual (2–3 minutes)

1   Place an imaginary book in front of you. In it is a brand-new story. No one has ever read or heard it before.
2   Open it at the first page. Write down the first three sentences of the story.
3   Now turn to page three, and run your finger down the page to the third paragraph.
4   Write the first three sentences of that paragraph.
5   Now turn over to the next page, on which is an illustration. Describe it.

6   Now turn to the last page and find the very last three sentences of the book. Write them.

7   Close the book. Look at the title on the front. Write the title of the book.

Exercise 10 Instant poem

Participants: All groups, individual (2–3 minutes)

1   I am a wizard and in a moment I will make all the words that exist in the world disappear except four words.

2   Choose the four words you are going to save and write them down.

3   I am a wizard and I have decided to be generous – you can keep four more words.

4   Choose them and write them down.

5   You now have eight words and they will soon be the only eight words in the world. If you turn those eight words into a poem, then all the other words will be saved.

6   You can repeat words if it helps the poem, but you can only use those eight.

Outcome

Well done, you've saved all the words in the world. I am no longer a wizard, but you are a poet.

Exercise 11 Responding to the word

Participants: All groups, individual (4–6 minutes)

Instant-writing can be liberating for any writer, and shows early-stage writers that to produce interesting phrases and original uses of words, they do not have to sit and stare at the sheet of paper waiting for inspiration. Indeed, 'waiting for inspiration' is the last thing we should be doing; the sitting and pondering comes very far down the line, when we are re-drafting and re-structuring work. The first task is to get it down, in whatever shape or form, in order to give our critical mind something to work on. This exercise takes us further along this path.

1   Draw a column down the left-hand side of a sheet of paper.

2   At the end of the exercise you will have a list of single words, which I will have given you.

3 You will write the first word in the column.

4 You will immediately write a short phrase or sentence (never just one word) – a thought, a question, a memory, a piece of nonsense – which the word sparks off for you.

5 Do not include the word itself in the phrase or sentence. (See Example 11.1.)

6 You have 10 seconds to write each response.

7 After 10 seconds you will move on to the second word. Stop writing the first phrase, write down the second word in the column, and start writing the second phrase.

8 Keep writing, don't plan, and if your mind goes blank just write 'I am writing I am writing' until something else arrives.

9 Here is the list: Green, Ice, Television, Red, Sand, Love, Religion, Banana, Telephone, Death, Dolphin, London, Shoe, Blue, Mother, Sea, Plane, Summer, Hamburger, Pink, War. (*Note to group leader:* I usually have a list of 20–25 words, with a good mix of colours, feelings, objects, abstracts and place-names. I never include pronouns. I always try to create a list of words which all members of the particular group will be familiar with.)

10 Read out some of the phrases. (See Examples 11.2.)

Example 11.1

If the word is 'green', I might write 'that tatty old school blazer' (because my school blazer was green and my mother sewed leather arm-patches on it).

Examples 11.2

Some phrases written by one group I worked with:

- *Green*: The Emerald City, I am writing, the city.
- *Love*: Pain and swelling, envy and blossoming.
- *Banana*: Ridicule and madness.
- *Telephone*: Revelations and gossip.
- *Death*: Darkness, sorrow, fear, I am writing I release.
- *War*: Dark, ragged edges, holes in fabric, tears.

Outcome

This exercise opens the door to a conversation about a very basic aspect of writing: that we all of us have our own individual ways of expressing ourselves through words. The description of 'war' as 'holes in fabric' is a brand new image of that event, unique to the person who wrote it. The exercise encourages the writers to trust their own inner voice, and to recognise that creating their own, original work – even if it is one phrase out of the 20–25 or so – is far more interesting than mimicking and reproducing what they have heard or read before. Once again, the 'instant' nature of the exercise means that they have had the experience of *doing it*, as opposed to *worrying about it*.

Exercise 12 Collective poems
Participants: All groups (10–20 minutes)

1   Take the first word from Exercise 11. Go round the circle and hear from the writers all their individual responses to it.

2   There is often much hilarity the first time around, so go back over the word again, this time asking the writers to speak a little more boldly and listening carefully to the different responses.

3   Discuss which images stand out vividly? What is the overall feel and mood? What lines work well next to each other?

4   Read around the circle again. Repeat the process for each word. What will emerge is a series of collectively created poems – the Green Poem, the Love Poem, etc. – each built on a range of individual perceptions.

Exercise 13 Poem into performance
Participants: All groups (10–20 minutes)

1   Read one of the poems from Exercise 12 again. Work on it in a bit more detail: it is now more than a random collection of written lines; it is a whole piece. What sort of mood and rhythm comes out? How do the lines sit with each other?

2   Everyone now writes down each line of the poem.

3   When the words 'I am writing I am writing' occur, keep these in as they are part of the poem.

4   Everyone now has the same copy of the collectively written poem. (See Example 13.1.)

5   Do the same thing with a few of the other words.

6   Divide up into small groups of 3–5. Each group takes one of the poems.

7   Devise a manner of presenting the poem, in whatever style you choose. Add movement, sound, repetition, choral speaking, etc., keeping in mind that the main aim is to bring the poems to life.

8   Share the results with the whole group.

Example 13.1

> The Emerald City, I am writing, the city
> Apples and trees and rain
> Trees and grass, I am writing I am
> Envy and sitting in a corner
> Grass and the grey clouds over the green
> ...

Outcome

Having gone through all the stages of Exercises 11 and 12, the group will now have had the experience of (a) individual writing, (b) collective writing, (c) working collaboratively in small groups, and (d) putting a piece of own-written text 'on its feet'.

Exercise 14 Instant writing, instant poems

Participants: Individual (4–6 minutes)

The work described in Exercises 12 and 13 is equally useful as a warm-up for any writer. Just flip through a dictionary, a magazine, or a novel, landing on words at random and write your responses. As ever, don't plan, don't pause, just write. By the end you will have your list of 20–25 phrases. Select the five most satisfying to you. Play with the order of them, creating a poem. Try doing this every day for a week: five days, five poems. What has that said about your week? What has it said about what you think? What has it said about how you write?

BUILDING A CHARACTER

Watching a play is a bit like observing a controlled experiment in human behaviour. The writer places characters together in a situation, just as the physicist mixes up elements and chemicals, to see what will happen. In both cases, explosions cannot be ruled out. It is no coincidence that a love-smitten person can speak of 'the chemistry that happened when we met'. Play-reviews speak of the 'on-stage chemistry' between the actors.

Some of the experiments in putting characters together in a story, to see what happens, are simple and predictable. In a sentimental romance, we know that the sweethearts will end up together. In a melodrama, we know that the hero will defeat the villain. Different genres of story delve into their characters at different levels: Little Red Riding Hood is much less complex than Hamlet; a character from an Agatha Christie story is likely to be more one-dimensional than one from Maya Angelou. All of them have one thing in common: they were built. Sometimes the foundations are shallow and we get the stereotype; with the best, the observation is deep and wholly original; but they all are based upon some form of research into the human heart and psyche.

How do we start building 'a character'? A key is the recognition that there are many sides to an individual. Hamlet continues to fascinate us, not because we know how the story ends (he and everyone else dies) but because, each time we hear it, we discover a new aspect to his character. Even Little Red Riding Hood (as we will see later on) may be more than 'the silly little girl who didn't listen to her mother's advice'.

I will start this series of exercises with three I developed specifically for use with the primary age group. However, as a reminder of the contradictions of human behaviour, and the fluidity of human nature, they are as revealing as many of the more complex exercises.

Exercise 15 Today my hand

Participants: Primary (1–3 minutes)

1 Draw the outline of your hand on a sheet of paper.

2 Think of all the things your hand has done today: ordinary things, things you feel good about, things you don't feel so good about, etc.

3 Around the hand write five sentences, each beginning with the words 'today my hand...'

4 Discuss all the different things a person's hand does in a day; how we don't even think about it, but how much it reveals about who we are and what we are like.

Outcome

This simple exercise shows how, in one day, the same person can do something with love ('...stroked my cat') and something not quite so loving ('...pulled my sister's hair'). It opens a conversation about how a character in a story may be many things, depending on who they are with, what they are doing, how they are feeling, etc.

Exercise 16 Inside–outside
Part one
Participants: Primary (3–6 minutes)

1   Think of someone you know and like. Write a physical description of them, so that if I were to meet them I would recognise them. Try and use all five senses. Are they big or small? What does their voice sound like? What sort of shoes do they wear? How do they walk, etc. (See Example 16.1.)

2   Draw a large outline of a person. This is an imaginary character. Around the outline, write as many physical descriptions as you can. Try and be very detailed. If they are wearing a blue shirt, is it bright blue or dark blue? If they have black hair, is it short, curly black hair or long, limp black hair? What are the different ways of describing the sound of a voice? We now have an idea of what that person is like on the outside. This tells us a little of who they are and what they might be like.

3   Now write inside the outline of the person. In the space where the head is, write down all the different words and phrases that describe 'thinking'. (See Examples 16.2.)

4   In the space where the heart is, write down all the words and phrases that describe 'feelings'. (See Examples 16.3.)

Example 16.1

He has rough hands, a high-pitched voice, shiny shoes, long legs, etc.

Examples 16.2

Plans, brainwork, thoughts, maths, ideas, interests, etc.

Examples 16.3

Love, sadness, hate, feeling good, jolly, etc.

Part two – inside–outside
Participants: Primary (3–6 minutes)

1   Draw a large outline of a person. This is now a character you are making up.

2   Using the list of 'inside things', write down what thoughts the person has, and what makes the person have different feelings.

Example 16.4

· She is interested in how big the universe is.
· She feels sad when she has to say goodbye to a friend.
· She thinks longer holidays are a good idea.
· She hates being told to go to bed.

Outcome

The 'outside' things give one description of the person, but the 'inside things' tell us much more about what a person might be like. When we are making characters for a story or a play, we need to imagine them from the outside; but it is even more important to imagine them from the inside.

Exercise 17 Action, feeling and thought

Participants: Primary (1 minute per story)

1   Having completed Exercise 16, go back to the hand in Exercise 15.
2   You have the original five things your hand did. The task now is to put a feeling to each of the five actions. (See Examples 17.1.)
3   You now have five very short stories, all containing an action and a feeling.
4   Now try and put a thought into the story as well. (See Examples 17.2.)
5   You now have five short stories, each including an action, a feeling and a thought.

Examples 17.1

· Today my hand pulled my sister's hair and *I felt guilty*.
· Today my hand stroked my cat and *I felt calm*.

Examples 17.2

· Today *I decided* to hurt my sister, so I pulled her hair, then I felt guilty.
· Today my hand stroked my cat. I felt calm and *I wondered* what the cat was thinking.

Outcome

- Exercises 15–17 all show that, in the creating of a character for a story, we need to know *what* is done (the hair was pulled), *why* it was done (the decision to hurt someone) and the *result* (the feeling of guilt).

- Interesting stories do not have to be copies of others you know. They can also start from things you know about, and develop on from there.

- Basic as these exercises are, they introduce to the very young the notion that stories – which come naturally to them anyway – can be developed and made even more interesting through working at them.

- The investigation of what goes on 'inside' is an invaluable way of extending the literacy of emotion, feeling and thought.

- The exercises open the door to a discussion about the consequences of actions, and the responsibility for our own feelings.

Exercise 18 Interviews

Participants: All groups (8–12 minutes)

As with many of the other early-stage exercises, the investigation into the question of how 'characters are built' can be helped by looking at our immediate surroundings; in this case, the people we are with.

1   Write a short list of questions you might ask someone if you were conducting an interview for a magazine: likes, dislikes, greatest fears, happiest moment, opinions on world events, etc.; questions you consider would give a wider public a thumbnail sketch of that person.

2   Work in pairs. Interview your partners (2–3 minutes each). Try not to get into general conversation.

3   If you find your interviewee is digressing into unhelpful anecdote, you may lead on to the next question.

4   Write down the answers in note form.

5   Write a 100-word paragraph on your partner, based upon your notes. Try and make it flow, as a magazine article would. You can rearrange things to fit the style of the article.

6   Rewrite the article, inserting a couple of facts or pieces of information that are fictional. Make them believable in terms of the person you are describing, but see if they can have a hint of drama, mystery, etc.

7   Read out the results. What fictional information seemed totally out of place with the general character being described? What fictional information was cleverly placed, as to seem totally in keeping with the person being described?

Outcome

This exercise can lead to a discussion about an essential element in the building of a character: whatever we invest the character with, it has to be credible. This does not mean to say that the quiet man down the road cannot turn out to be a mass-murderer; but only if we can say 'of course ...that makes sense of everything we know about him' when we discover the awful truth.

Exercise 19 Name and character
Part one
Participants: Primary

You are going to create a character for a story. The character is not like anyone you know. You are going to start by finding a name for them. The name might be one you have heard before, or it might be one that has never been heard before.

1   Write down your own name.

2   Write out the letters of your name on separate small squares of paper.

3   Rearrange any of the letters to make new names.

4   Write out the list of new names.

5   Choose one of the names for the character you are going to write about. It can often be more interesting to choose a name that has never been heard of before. (See Examples 19.1.)

6   Find more about the character by using Exercises 16–18.

Examples 19.1

•   *Noel*: Leo, Leon, Len, Eno, Lon, etc.

•   *Charlotte*: Lotte, Carl, Cloe, Chloe, Atto, Tote, etc.

Part two – name and character
Participants: Primary

You can use the character's name to discover more about them.

1 Write your own name in a column down the side of the paper.

2 Write a list of things you like, beginning with each letter of the name. (See Example 19.2.)

3 Write a list of things you don't like, again beginning with each letter of the name. (See Example 19.3.)

4 Repeat the exercise, using one of the new names you made from your own name.

5 If you are working in a group, discuss all the new characters. What clues as to who they might be are given by the 'likes' and 'don't likes'?

Example 19.2

Things I like.

· N: Newspapers.
· O: Oranges.
· E: Elephants.
· L: Lightning.

Example 19.3

Things I don't like.

· N: Nightmares.
· O: Oil-spills.
· E: Envy.
· L: Ladders.

Exercise 20 Characteristics

Participants: All groups, individual (4 minutes)

Definition of 'characteristic': 'a distinguishing quality, attribute or trait'; that is, moods, emotions, and ways of behaving that you associate with a person.

1 Write a list of single words you might use to describe qualities of character in a person. (See Examples 20.1.)

2 Look at the list. Find pairs of words that seem to contradict each other. Write thumbnail character sketches in which the person is described as having a range of characteristics. (See Examples 20.2.)

Examples 20.1

Daft, wise, funny, angry, witty, unpredictable, bossy, helpful, etc.

Examples 20.2

• He's daft, but he's wise.

• She may be bossy, but she's helpful.

• Sometimes she's angry and unpredictable, but she's wise.

Outcome

A 'daft' person might be interesting in a story, as might a 'wise' person. But a person who is 'daft but wise' is going to be very interesting. Shakespeare's clowns are often the wisest characters in the plays.

Exercise 21 Type

Participants: All groups, individual (5 minutes)

Definition of 'type': 'a person who typifies a particular quality'. This is slightly different from 'characteristic' in that it suggests that the quality identified is more central to the way the person is generally.

1   Write a list of popular or common phrases that are used to describe what type of person a character is. (See Examples 21.1.)

2   Using the 'daft but wise' examples in Exercise 20, create descriptions of characters that include (a) two 'characteristic' words and (b) 'type' phrases. (See Examples 21.2.)

3   Write a list of phrases that characters might use to describe them-selves. (See Examples 21.3.)

Examples 21.1

• She's a natural born leader.

• He's a real creep.

• She's slippery as an eel.

• That one's a bit high-and-mighty.

• She's a real sport.

• He's a proper tyrant.

• He's always got his head in the clouds.

Examples 21.2

- He's daft but wise and he always gets his own way.
- She may be bossy, but she's helpful and she's a real sport.

Examples 21.3

- I never let life get me down.
- I always tread carefully in life.
- A born optimist, me.
- I'm out for number one.
- Whatever life sends my way, I take it on the chin.

Outcome

- We have now begun to explore the possibility that a 'character' may have different sides to them, often contradictory ones. Their 'type' may be the dominant expression of how they are, but that may contain many other shades and variations.
- In a play, people describe other people. They also describe themselves. The two might be very contradictory. As we shall see in Chapter 4, what characters say about themselves may be very much at odds with what someone else says about them.

Exercise 22 What's in a name?

Participants: All groups, individual (5–10 minutes)

You will eventually put a name to all the characters in your play or story. This is no light matter; no lighter than when your own parents or guardians gave you a name. We are very much defined by our names and they are centrally bound up with our self-identity and our personal history. It is no coincidence that when oppressors decide to eradicate the identities of those they oppress, one of the first things they often do is eradicate original names. The slave-owners in America gave their slaves westernised names; in 1930s Germany, all Jewish women had to register under the name of 'Sarah'. How about all those true stories of people wanting to make a new life for themselves, and in doing so have changed their names?

All this may seem very far from the question of how to build a character for a fictional story, but an examination of our own names throws a great deal of light upon that matter, and this is what this exercise is based upon. A friend once sent me a birthday card with an African saying on it: 'If you can walk you can dance, if you can talk you can sing.' I add a third thing: 'If you can write your name you can tell a story.'

1   Write your name and the things you know and feel about it. (See Example 22.1.)

2   Take from your account of your name a few elements that feel key and use them to create a poem, reordering them in a manner that feels satisfying. In this way, you will have created a boiled-down *essence* of 'you'. (See Example 22.2.)

Example 22.1

Whenever I use this exercise, I always begin by using my own name as an example of what I mean when I say that 'name' and 'character' are very linked. Here is a rather full account; I generally do not use it in full, but draw from it as appropriate to the context I am working in.

- My name is Noël Greig.

- Noel is the French word for Christmas. In other languages it is Nowell (Old English), Manuel (Spanish), Emmanuel (Hebrew), Nollaig (Celtic), Manolis (Greek). They are all variants on 'First Born'.

- I was given my name because I was born on Christmas Day, 1944, the last year of the Second World War.

- Famous names I share a birthday with: the film star Humphrey Bogart and Jesus Christ.

- I didn't like my name when I was young. No one else in the small town where I grew up shared it and it made me feel a bit exposed, particularly at Christmas when the school sang the carol 'The First Noel', which made me blush, which is why I still blush easily. The name Noel also sounded a bit like a girl's name and – at that time in my life – it made me feel uncomfortable; even more so when, in adolescence, I came to realise I was gay. My name seemed a real giveaway, at a time when to be gay was, to say the least, frowned upon.

- On the other hand (and in complete contradiction to the above) I liked the name because it did make me feel 'special' (perhaps even with a bit of a 'Jesus Christ complex', in wanting to put the world to rights). The fact that there was a famous playwright, Noel Coward, with whom I shared my name, added to this feeling. Although when I discovered he was gay (before I'd come out) this became more problematic.

- I've had various nicknames: Nollie, Noelie, Nelly. I like them all, because they remind me of the affection with which friends have used them.

- My second name (my paternal name) derives from the Scottish clan MacGregor.

- When the clan was outlawed for rising up against the English, the clan-name and the speaking of Gaelic was banned, and families chose variants of Greg, Gregg, Greig, etc. Many of them emigrated to other lands to escape English oppression. It may be that the Norwegian composer Edward Grieg may have had similar origins.

- People are always spelling and pronouncing my name wrong (Grieg as in -eeg, not Greig as in -egg), which makes me very angry. I remember one teacher at infant school who punished me for telling her that she had got my name wrong. To this day I still feel outraged by that incident.

Example 22.2

Here is an example of the list of thoughts and feelings turned into a poem, written by a nine-year old pupil in a class I worked with in a school in Nottingham.

> I don't know what my name means
> I would like my name to mean great
> I think my name's colour is blue
> I think my name's shape is square
> I think my name's animal is dog
> My name comes from Vietnam
> My name is common in Vietnam
> I quite like my name
> I don't know why I was named Minh
> I think my name's sound is the beat of a drum
> My name sounds like win
> It also sounds like my mum's name Lihn
> I think my name's food would be rice

Outcome

Simply by using our names as the controlling factor, we have revealed quite a lot about ourselves. Nine-year old Minh's view on himself uses a lot of imagery, while mine was more autobiographical, but both include personal history, family history, ethnic origins, etc. The exercise reveals a huge amount about what we mean by 'creating a character': our fictional characters need to have as rich a history as our own lives have. Just as our own stories can be told through our names, so too should the stories of our fictional characters. We have seen how 'character' and 'story' are inextricably linked.

Exercise 23 Celebrating the name

Participants: All groups (10–15 minutes)

This is a direct follow-up to Exercise 22. Simply miss out the very last stage – the writing of the poem about yourself.

1   In pairs, read over the notes you have made on your names. Talk about them for a few minutes, then swap them over.

2   Now go and sit away from your partner. (This is important, to ensure that no more conversation takes place.)

3   Drawing from what your partner has written, you are going to create a poem celebrating their name. It will be about five or six lines long, so you will be selecting from all the things written. Select those lines, images, turns of phrase, etc., which you feel gives a sense of the person – an *essence* of them. You may add some words if it helps, and you may place things in a different order; but always remember that you are using what your partner has given you, and that you are celebrating their name.

4   Give or read the poem to your partner, as a gift. Post it up around the room.

5   Which images 'capture' a person well?

Outcome

Exercises 22 and 23 touch on an aspect of 'character-creating' that I will deal with later on: the capturing of the *essence* of a character. By boiling-down the material to a few lines, you have been getting to the heart of what the person is like, of what makes them unique in your view.

The 'name-poem' is also an invaluable tool for developing creative interaction between individuals and groups. I first used it when working on a project which 'twinned' a primary class in the UK with another in Singapore. The pupils worked at long-range, starting with the exchange of thoughts on their names and then the poems. This created the basis for really creative dialogue between two very different groups. Used in a culturally mixed group, it is also an excellent tool for developing bridges of understanding and interest. (See Chapter 9 for details of this project.)

Even 'not knowing' about a name can be useful, as it offers a splendid context for research: genealogy, geography, history, etc.

FINDING THE STORY

Definition of 'story': 'in the every day sense, any narrative or tale recounting a series of events'. A good test of good story is to see if it can be 'boiled down' to the essence of what it recounts. Some examples:

- *Romeo and Juliet:* Two young people from warring families fall in love, everything is against them, their attempts to make it right fail, they die and everyone feels responsible and resolve to make peace.
- *Little Red Riding Hood:* A young girl strays off the path, against her mother's advice, meets a wolf, gets her grandmother eaten by the wolf and is rescued in the end.
- *An episode of Eastenders:* The barmaid falls in love with her husband's brother and there are fisticuffs in the pub. She decides she loves her husband best.

These examples are stories that take place in highly fictional worlds, – I include television soap operas such as Eastenders and Coronation Street, and there is nothing wrong with that. However, in researching the question 'what makes a story work?', it is again useful to consider the world immediately around us. The reference to 'the every day' in the dictionary definition is useful, for in fact we tell stories all the time; it comes naturally to us: gossip, anecdote, 'tall stories' and downright lies, reminiscence, jokes, instructions, etc. Think of all the phrases we use to describe and comment on our story-telling activities: 'he's spinning you a line', 'the whole truth and nothing but the truth', 'that's a pack of lies', 'it's the same old story', 'now just you listen to me', etc.

The playwright Bertolt Brecht wrote a series of poems on the theatre and the telling of stories. In one of them ('On Everyday Theatre') he advises actors to remember that their story-telling art is based upon an activity that happens daily – gossip, telling tales, reporting incidents and accidents, telling jokes, lying, etc. – and that they should never forget that link with the real world, beyond the artificial one of the theatre. As writers, it is useful to take on board Brecht's advice: there are stories being told around us all the time and we have always that source of riches to draw from.

Exercise 24 Everyday stories
Participants: Individual (24 hours)

Keep a notebook with you for 24 hours. Jot down all the ways in which you hear (or tell) stories, or snatches of stories, over that period. Don't include stories from the TV, radio or the papers, just those you hear live, at home, work, school, on the bus, in the shop, etc.

Exercise 25 Instant stories

Participants: All groups, individual (30 seconds each)

1 Write down these three things: daffodil, cat, kitchen.
2 Write a sentence that links all three things into a very short story, keeping them in the same order. Make the story *active*. Begin with the words 'Yesterday...'. (See Example 25.1.)
3 Try these:

   • Banana, football, telephone.
   • Tree, pen, river.
   • Television, chicken, bed.
   • Computer, crocodile, toast.
   • Book, shoe, penguin.

4 Try different openings:

   • 'Today I would like to...'
   • 'I don't understand why...'
   • 'The world would be a better place if...'. (See Examples 25.2.)

Example 25.1

Yesterday I picked a daffodil, but the cat ate it and then was sick in the kitchen.

Examples 25.2

• Today I would like to put a banana-skin under the football-captain's shoe, then telephone the papers to say I've taken his place.

• The world would be a better place if we could look at a tree and write a poem about it with a pen, instead of chopping it down and sending it to the sawmill down the river.

• I don't understand why the computer gave all the information about the crocodile but it didn't stop me burning the toast.

Outcome

Writing creates meaning. By putting known words together in new ways, we create new meanings, new images, and new expressions. What do computers, crocodiles and toast have to do with each other? This exercise has shown how, by linking together things that do not seem to belong together, we can create narratives that have not been heard before.

Exercise 26 What happens next?

Participants: All groups, individual (10–15 minutes)

All stories invite us to ask questions. The basic 'What happens next?' is as much at the heart of Oedipus Rex as it is for Little Red Riding Hood. The more complex the story, the more complex the questions. With Little Red, we want to know if she'll escape the jaws of the wolf. The plight of Oedipus raises huge, possibly unanswerable questions around our human inability, or refusal, to recognise the signs of the disasters awaiting us.

The best questions are often the ones that prompt other questions. The construction of a play can be regarded as the process of the writer setting themselves questions, then seeing what others they lead to.

1   Invent a character very quickly, using some of the methods in the earlier exercises. Jot down two or three things about the character: what they do, what characteristic they may have, what type of person they are. (See Example 26.1.)

2   Write down a question about the character. It can be a 'big question' or a 'small question'. (See Examples 26.2.)

3   Write down three or four questions that are prompted by the first question. (See Examples 26.3.)

4   Don't attempt to answer any of the questions. For each single question, find three or four more that are prompted by it. By the end you will have about twenty-or-so questions (big and small) about your character: who they are and what they are doing in life.

5   Select those questions that seem most useful in suggesting a story. Don't even attempt to think about what the story might be. All you are doing is exploring the question 'what happens next?'.

6   Try following each of these opening questions with five or six others:
  •   Why is the student playing truant?
  •   Where has the nurse hidden the medicine?
  •   Who does the elderly woman want to see?
  •   What is the soldier bringing home from the war?

Example 26.1

He is a bank manager. He is curious but cautious. He doesn't suffer fools gladly.

Examples 26.2

- What is the bank manager's big secret? (big question)
- What did the bank manager have for breakfast today? (small question)

Examples 26.3

- Who suspects that the bank manager has got something to hide? What mistake did the bank manager make? Why is the bank manager scared?
- Where did the bank manager have his breakfast? Did the bank manager finish his breakfast? What was the bank manager thinking about when he *was* eating his breakfast?

Exercise 27 The shape of the story

Participants: All groups, individual

All narratives have a shape, and we will be looking at this in detail in Chapter 8. Here is an exercise that explores one shape (a circular story). It may be used as a model for a group, or an individual, to create a succession of small, linked stories.

1 Sit in a circle. If you are working on your own, draw a large circle.

2 Around the circle are a number of characters in a story. We don't know anything about them.

3 Select an everyday object that has a number of uses. Make it an object that can be easily held in the hand. Discuss what the object can be used for (its primary use and secondary uses). (See Example 27.1.)

4 Write a list of all the different ways that an object may change hands. (See Examples 27.2.)

5 The object is going to travel clockwise around the circle, until it returns to the starting point.

6 Each time the object changes hands, describe or write down (a) what it is being used for and/or (b) how it comes to change hands. (See Examples 27.3.)

7   You have now completed the 'journey of the object'. You have also discovered – through the things that happened around the object – the beginning of some dramatic situations. Explore a few of those in brief note form. What strong dramatic episodes can you suggest? (See Example 27.4.)

8   Discuss or make notes on how each episode of the story could be extended into a short scene.

Example 27.1

A pair of scissors:

- Cutting things: hair, paper, cloth, string, pastry, vegetables, etc.

- Getting tops of bottles, piercing tin cans, etc.

- Emergency uses: as a screwdriver, as a hole-punch, etc.

- Making marks: carving a name on a tree, scratching a message on a door, etc.

- Injuring and killing. (The rule here is that the scissors can only be used once for this purpose, and this may happen in the very final exchange.)

Examples 27.2

Stolen, lost, given as a gift (birthday, wedding, etc.), sold, bartered, thrown away, confiscated, exchanged, pawned, etc.

Examples 27.3

- Character A is cutting character B's hair. When character B leaves the premises, she sneaks the scissors into her handbag.

- Character B is at the airport. The scissors are in her hand luggage. At security, character C confiscates the scissors and pockets them for himself.

- Character C realises he has forgotten character D's birthday. He hurriedly wraps the scissors up, then gives them to character D.

Example 27.4

We see character B having her hair cut in the salon by character A. Character A is not paying much attention to the job and is boasting about his recent holiday. Character B is clearly unhappy with the results, but character A insists that he has done a good job. Character B pays up, reluctantly, then puts the scissors in her handbag while character A is at the till.

Outcome

The process of writing is one of setting problems and attempting to solve them. We make narratives by asking questions. The deeper the questions, the more complex and satisfying the story will be for the audience.

DIALOGUE

When we read a play, the first thing we are aware of is the dialogue – and the amount of it. 'It's the writing of the dialogue that really scares me' is something I've often heard said; and of course, the notion of the blank sheet of paper (or screen) sitting there, waiting for 'dialogue' to land on it, is terrifying. Usually though, plays don't happen like that and, as a general principle, situation, story and character all form themselves in the writer's head before the dialogue emerges. Bits of speech, snatches of conversations, turns of phrase might emerge along the way, but fully formed scenes can only flow easily and naturally from a strong story based upon developed characters.

Even though dialogue often comes last, it is useful at the start of any process to have a sense of being able to write it. These exercises can be done on your own, or with a partner. As ever, don't plan, just write.

Exercise 28 Alphabet-dialogue
Participants: All groups, individual (5–8 minutes)

1   At the top of the page, write out the alphabet.

2   You are going to write a dialogue between two people. You do not know who they are, where they are or what is happening.

3   Begin each sentence with a letter of the alphabet, starting with **A** and proceeding through to **Z**. (See Example 28.1.)

4   For **Q**, **X** and **Z** you can break the rule: if you can't find a word beginning with the letter, it can appear somewhere in the word.

5   See what clues the A–Z dialogue gives and what questions it prompts: Who might the two characters be? What could their relationship be? What things might happen in the story? What might the story be about? (See Example 28.2.)

Example 28.1

Here is part of a dialogue created by a member of a college-group I ran a few years back:

One: Anyone can swim. By human nature.
Two: Can't be bothered really.
One: Don't give me that. Everybody can do it, I've said that already.
Two: Forget what you've said, you're wrong.
One: Gordon can't swim, he'd sink.
Two: How do you know Gordon?
One: I just do.
Two: Just is a very inexact word.
One: Kitchen is inexact, what's your point?
Two: Leave it off, OK? Mind your own business.
One: No, come on, tell me.
    ...

Example 28.2

On the basis of the eleven lines quoted, we might suggest: they are two friends, they have quite a competitive relationship, they have a rivalry over Gordon, there might later be a tragic incident involving swimming, and the story might be about friendship.

Outcome

The 'limitation' of the alphabet-task serves a number of functions:

- As a task-driven exercise, it removes any worries about 'writing dialogue' by requiring the writer to focus on the task.

- It gives a structure within which the dialogue has to operate. A–Z is, of course, a rudimentary structure; but – as we shall see – a scene in a play is something that leads to a definite outcome. However brief the scene, it will always have its 'A' and its 'Z' in terms of how it needs to start and when it needs to conclude.

- It establishes the notion that the writing of dialogue is not about reproducing how people talk 'in real life'. We may hear things that people do say in 'real life' and use them in our writing; but dialogue in plays is artificially constructed. Writers draw upon modes of conversational-exchange that exist, but no one speaks in exactly the way as the characters in a play by Oscar Wilde, a monologue by Samuel Beckett, or an episode of Eastenders. The cleverness of all of them – whether you like them or not – is that they 'sound real'.

Exercise 29 Place-association dialogue
Participants: All groups, individual (5–8 minutes)

1 Think of the city, town, etc., where you live.
2 Write down five locations, five colours and five things (animal, vegetable or mineral) you associate with the place. (You could make the list longer by adding other categories: feelings, abstracts, etc.) (See Example 29.1.)
3 Rewrite the list, in alphabetical order (first letters only). (See Example 29.2.)
4 Write a dialogue in which the words occur in exactly that order. Once again, you do not know who the characters are when you start. See if the associations with the location begin to give a sense of who they might be, or what might be going on. (See Example 29.3.)

Example 29.1

Brighton: Pier, Marina, Pavilion, Station, Beach, Green, Turquoise, Grey, White, Cream, Pebbles, Litter, Driftwood, Seagulls, Chewing gum.

Example 29.2

Beach, Cream, Chewing gum, Driftwood, Green, Grey, Litter, Marina, Pier, Pavilion, Pebbles, Station, Seagulls, Turquoise, White.

Example 29.3

A: Do you fancy a walk down the **b**each?
B: Only if you'll buy me an ice **c**ream.
A: I paid for the **c**hewing gum, it's your turn now.
B: **D**riftwood! That's all I am to you. **G**reen stuff, **g**rey stuff, I'm just a bit of **l**itter chucked up by the sea.
A: Who paid for that meal down the **M**arina? Who paid for the rides on the **P**ier?
     Etc.

Exercise 30 Filling in the gaps
Participants: All groups, individual (2–3 minutes)

1 Here are three lines of dialogue:
     Your mother used to visit this place.

> Please don't break it.
> Here they come.

2   You have two or three characters.

3   Briefly examine the lines for clues: who, where, what, etc.

4   Write a short exchange of dialogue. The three lines should appear at points in the dialogue, in the order I have given them. (See Example 30.1.)

5   Try these:

> I'm so lonely these days.
> My bedroom needs painting.
> I think it was a blue flower.
>
> *and*
>
> The dog lay on the bed.
> You catch the train at teatime.
> It was inside the paper bag.

Example 30.1

A: Before she died, your mother used to visit this place. She loved this place.

B: Dad, you made a promise never to talk about her. Please don't break it.

A: I can't help it, every time we come here...

B: Here they come, the tears...

Exercise 31 Word-lists

Participants: All groups, individual (5–6 minutes)

We have already used lists of words as a channel for the imagination. Here they can be used to create a dialogue out of thin air.

1   Use this list of words: blue, fire, television, ice, car, green, love, rain, food, hand, mother, banana, history, song, war, home, red, newspaper, hope, tree.

2   Write a dialogue for two people. You don't know who they are or what the situation is. The words should occur in the dialogue in exactly the same order as they appear in the list. 'Blue' appears first, 'fire' comes next, etc. Once you have used a word, it can appear again at any point in the dialogue.

3   Don't plan, just launch in with the first line and see where the words lead you.

Example 31.1

One: I saw a sheep that had **blue** dye on it.

Two: Yeah, maybe it got burnt in a **fire** with blue flames.

One: It could have rubbed up against a **television** when that blue movie was on.

Two: Or someone could've spilt some of that blue **ice** drink on it.

One: I spray painted my **car** blue, then I got some on my leg – does that make me a sheep?

Two: Your car is **green**.

One: You're avoiding the question. I **love** it when you do that. Tell me if you think I'm a sheep.

Two: Well, stand out in the **rain** and if your skin shrinks, then maybe you are a sheep. And if you are a sheep I'll give you a **hand** to find some grass.

...

Exercise 32 One-to-ten dialogue

Participants: All groups, individual (2–3 minutes)

1 You have two people. You don't know who they are.

2 There will be ten lines of dialogue. You don't know what they will be.

3 The first line will have ten words, the second nine words and so on, up to the tenth line, which will have one word.

Example 32.1

A: Have you got any bananas for sale today, mister Smith? (10)

B: Sorry, I don't have bananas, but I've got apples. (9)

A: Those apples you sold last week were rotten. (8)

B: So are you calling me a cheat? (7)

...

Outcome

With the above exercises, we have established a principle that is at the heart of the development of all stories: even the most basic text contains within it the potential seeds for further development. When working with writers on their plays, I have found that the best way of moving forward is to address the clues that the text already provides. We all have a tendency to push aside an early thought or idea; to dismiss it as not very interesting. But an idea becomes interesting only if it is worked on, so it is important is to keep digging away, right up to the point where we absolutely *know* it must be discarded. And even then, there might still be something that is useful. What we must do is to place value on the fact that *anything* we commit to the written word has value and potential.

PLOT

Although we have just dipped into work on dialogue, this often comes last in the making of a play. Character, situation and story generally come before full dialogue is developed. This applies to someone writing a full-length play, a group devising a sketch, or a pupil taking part in a half-hour writing session in primary school. Get the story-idea, explore what-happens-to-who, then show it through what is spoken. If you did the 'bank manager questions' in Exercise 26, you have already begun to explore this area.

We will be looking in detail at different aspects of the word 'story' later on; for the moment, let's focus a little more on the 'what-happens-next' aspect – or 'plot'.

> **Plot**: the pattern of events and situations in a narrative or dramatic work, as selected and arranged both to emphasise relationship – usually of cause and effect – between incidents and to elicit a particular kind of interest in the reader or audience, such as surprise or suspense.
>
> (Oxford Dictionary of Literary Terms)

The very word itself tells us everything: we 'plot revenge', we 'plot the points on the map'. If 'story' is the total picture, plot is about the detail-moments of the story: the 'plot-points' as they are called.

Exercise 33 Journey: door-to-door
Participants: All groups, individual (10–15 minutes)

1   If you are working away from home, think of the journey you made between your own front door and the door of the building you are in. If you are working at home, go for a walk and come back.

2   Write down, in order, about ten things that you saw, heard or did along the way. Think of the journey as a washing line, with the ten things pegged out along it. In the story of your journey, these are your 'plot-points'. (See Example 33.1.)

3 It is quite likely that your journey was, like mine, quite uneventful and routine. So look along the washing-line and find somewhere to insert one thing that *didn't* happen. As with the exercise on 'character' earlier, keep it within the bounds of what you have set up. (See Example 33.2.)

4 Consider what possibilities are offered by the event that didn't happen: something unusual, mysterious, alarming, thought-provoking.

5 Bring another person, related to the new event, into the story at this point. Make it something that is believable within the world you have described – avoid getting carried away by men from Mars, gruesome murders or encounters with film stars.

6 Rewrite the final part of the story from the new event. Allow it to go where it needs to; but you will always end by entering the door you are travelling towards. (See Example 33.3.)

7 Write a list of questions you would like the story so far to answer.

8 Write a list of things that might happen next.

9 Write a short dialogue for two of the characters.

Example 33.1

Here is what happened to me this morning:

- I left my house to go to the shops.
- I looked at the sea.
- I walked past the park and looked at the autumn trees.
- It started to rain, so I sheltered in the porch of a block of flats.
- I decided to roll a cigarette but the papers were wet.
- I was beginning to wish I'd never come out.
- The rain was blowing into the porch so I carried on walking.
- A car drove into a puddle and splashed me.
- The sun came out suddenly.
- At the shop I bought some yoghurt and bread.
- I decided to buy a bar of chocolate to cheer myself up.
- I arrived back at my home.

Example 33.2

Everything stays the same until it starts to rain:

- It started to rain, so I sheltered in the porch of a block of flats.
- There was a brand new umbrella propped up by the door.
- I was about to take it when someone came out of the flats.

Example 33.3

- There was a brand new umbrella propped up by the door.
- I was about to take it when a man came out of the flats.
- The man accused me of being a thief and walked away with the umbrella.
- An elderly woman came out of the flats, looking for her umbrella.
- I explained that someone had taken it.
- She became very upset.
- She explained that there was a man in the flats harassing her and stealing her things.
- I gave her my phone number. I said I would phone the police on her behalf.
- She went back inside.
- I tried to roll a cigarette, but the papers were wet.
- Etc.

Outcome

This exercise shows us that we don't have to go far from our own front door to find the makings of a story. Forget men from Mars, murders and film stars, just look around your own daily life and invent from there. Keep your inventions true to the world of the story and then, if you really *must* have little green men or Madonna appearing, it is more likely that they will have a proper function in the story.

The exercise also introduces an important element in building a story, which we will be looking at later: the placing of an incident, somewhere quite near the beginning, which *makes the story happen*. In the example, by bringing in the woman who is being harassed, the possibility of dramatic events stemming from the meeting is set up.

Exercise 34 Plot and dialogue

Participants: All groups (15–20 minutes)

1 Divide up into small groups of four or five.
2 Each group is a 'family'.
3 Decide which member of the family each person is.
4 The 'family' is doing something ordinary together. You could choose something domestic (at home watching the TV), but think of all the

other possibilities: having a picnic in the park, watching a carnival parade, etc.

5 You are going to create a progression of frozen 'plot-moments' that will show a story. These will take the form of still images – rather like a sequence of snapshots. The story is about how a conflict arises and is finally resolved. Avoid getting into physical conflict and focus on what is happening psychologically.

6 The sequence is as follows:

- The family is engaged in its activity.
- There is a minor upset – a misunderstanding or a disagreement.
- There is a conflict into which everyone is drawn.
- Attempts are made to resolve the conflict.
- The conflict is finally resolved. (See Example 34.1.)

7 Share the results with the whole group.

8 Replay one of the sequences. This time, as each frozen moment is shown, imagine there is a blank 'speech-bubble' above each of the character's heads.

9 The audience now suggests what is in the speech-bubbles. (See Example 34.2.)

10 Repeat this process for all the sequences.

11 Each 'family' group will now write out the script. Use the suggestions from the 'speech-bubble' exercise, but allow the story to develop. Fill in the gaps between the main plot-events.

Example 34.1

- The family is having a picnic on the beach.
- The grandfather won't let the little daughter go into the sea.
- Everyone takes sides.
- The father suggests they all go for a paddle.
- They all take off their shoes, walk down to the sea and paddle.

Example 34.2

Frozen image 1: The family is having a picnic on the beach.

Daughter: When we've finished eating, are we going to go in the water?

Mother: I was reading in the paper that it's not very clean.

Son: Can I have another banana?

Father: You've had two already, that last one's for your sister.
Grandfather: Ah, this is the life.
                Etc.

Frozen image 2: The grandfather won't let the little daughter into the sea.

Daughter: I'm going to go in the sea.
Father: Eat your banana first.
Grandfather: You stay here, my girl, you're not going in that filthy muck.
Son: Yes, it's filthy muck.
Mother: Yes, it did say in the paper...
                Etc.

Outcome

We have now seen how dialogue supports a succession of plot-events. If we know the shape of the story, and where the main dramatic moments are, the dialogue will begin to naturally fill out that shape.

THEME

If plot is about the details of 'what happens', then theme is about 'about'.

> **Theme:** a salient abstract idea that emerges from a literary work's treatment of its subject matter. While the subject of a work is described concretely in terms of its action (e.g. 'the adventures of a newcomer in the big city'), its theme or themes will be described in more abstract terms (e.g. love, war, revenge, betrayal, fate, etc.). The theme of a work may be announced explicitly, but more often it emerges indirectly through the recurrence of motifs.
>
> (Oxford Dictionary of Literary Terms)

The theme of Macbeth could be: 'the journey of a man from honour to dishonour.' The theme of Little Red Riding Hood could be: 'the journey of a child from the safety of home to the dangers of the wide world.'

Exercise 35 Theme from lists: monologues
Participants: All groups, individual (10–15 minutes)

1   Write out a list of 20–25 words, under the following categories:

    •   Eleven 'things' (animal, vegetable, mineral; natural or human-made; no people).

- Six colours.
- Five feelings or emotions. (See Example 35.1.)

2   Now re-write the list, mixing the categories up by placing the words in alphabetical order (taking only the first letter of the word as the guide, that is, all the A-words, then all the B-words, etc.). (See Example 35.2.)

3   Write a speech on a particular theme or something that is quite important, such as *'war'*. There are two rules: your particular theme cannot be mentioned by name, and the words in the list must all appear absolutely in that order. The first one to appear must be 'ant', the last one 'zoo'. (See Example 35.3.)

4   Once again, the advice is not to plan; just launch in and allow the words to lead you. These key words are the spine, and the other words you use are the bridges between them. Do not worry if it doesn't seem to be making 'logical sense' – indeed, if it seems completely illogical and off-the-wall and if it makes you laugh, then so much the better.

5   Try using the same list of words to explore other themes: *education, AIDS, loyalty, guilt, trust, etc.* Never mention the word in your writing; allow the word to help you find your images and expressions.

6   After using the same list for all the above exercises, reflect on how the imposition of different themes stimulate the creation of fresh, new imagery.

Example 35.1

Gun, Ant, Eiffel Tower, Moon, Desk, Cat, Grass, Answerphone, Bluebell, Zoo, Mat, Red, Green, Blue, Yellow, Pink, Black, Envy, Joy, Love, Hate, Misery.

Example 35.2

Ant, Answerphone, Bluebell, Blue, Black, Cat, Desk, Eiffel Tower, Envy, Gun, Grass, Green, Hate, Joy, Love, Mat, Misery, Moon, Pink, Red, Yellow, Zoo.

Example 35.3

I gave a writer the list we have above and asked her to write a short story on the theme of *'war'*. So what do an ant, an answerphone and a bluebell have to do with war? She came up with this opening: 'The ant crawled across the mud towards the body. In the dead man's hand was an answerphone. By his foot was a crushed bluebell...'.

A beautiful example of creating a fresh new image of war, through three words which did not seem to belong together at all.

Exercise 36 Theme from lists: dialogues

Participants: All groups, individual (3–4 minutes each)

Using the same list of words, write a dialogue for two people, around the following themes: *betrayal, revenge, bullying, death*. Once again, the theme should not be mentioned by name, and the words should occur in the dialogue in the same order as in the list. Keep in mind the fact that although there is one theme (never mentioned by name), the characters may display very different attitudes towards it.

Outcome

What these exercises show is that a theme can be 'talked around', often in illuminating and poetic ways, in a manner quite different from an academic essay on a subject. Once again, the 'limitation' of a list becomes the stimulation to a creative angle on the topic in hand.

LOCATION

The location of the story – where it takes place – crucial to the telling of the tale. As we shall see later on, the location is much more than the backdrop to the narrative, and the seed of a story can be found in where it is set.

Exercise 37 The object and the place

Participants: All groups, individual (5–10 minutes)

1   Think of an ordinary object.
2   Put it somewhere in the world where it doesn't normally belong. (See Example 37.1)
3   Ask questions about the image. Don't try to answer them. (See Example 37.2.)
4   Consider the questions. Now think about 'what happened before?'. Ask a few more questions. (See Example 37.3.)

Example 37.1

Image: A television set is half-way up a mountain.

Example 37.2

- Where is the mountain and what does it look like?
- What time of day or year is it?
- What is the weather like?
- What type of television set is it?
- What condition is the television set in?
- Etc.

Example 37.3

If this particular television set is up this particular mountain, in this sort of weather on this sort of day, and in this sort of condition, then:

- How did it get there?
- Who did it belong to?
- Where is that person now?
- Did they put the television set on the mountain?
- Did someone else put it there?
- Why did they put it on the mountain?
- Is there something special about this mountain: its history, the myths and stories about it, where it is located?
- Etc.

Outcome

We have begun to see that the 'location' can begin to become a character in its own right. As we will see later, the location can be an active participant in the story. You need to research and imagine your location as thoroughly as you do the characters.

END OF THE DAY

When you are working with a group, it can be useful to round off the session with work that gathers some of the strands together. Here are some suggestions.

Exercise 38 Writing is...
Participants: All groups, individual (1 minute)

Write as many phrases as you can, each beginning with the words 'writing is...'

Exercise 39 Instant ingredients
Participants: All groups, individual (3–5 minutes)

You have just been asked to write a play for your local theatre. The only problem is, they want some information about it right away. If you can produce the following ingredients in the next few minutes, they will produce the play:

1   The names of the two main characters and a little about them.
2   The story and some of the key plot developments.
3   The theme and how that will develop.
4   The setting and how it will affect the action.

Exercise 40 Pleasing the actors
Participants: All groups, individual (2–3 minutes)

Your local theatre are going to produce your play, and they have two major actors to perform in it. The only problem is, the actors want to have an example of some of the dialogue they will be given. If you can produce some really original dialogue from the play in the next few minutes, the actors will agree to be in the play. Use Exercise 30.

Exercise 41 One minute plays
Participants: All groups, individual (1 minute each)

1   The play starts with 'Hello' and ends with 'Goodbye'. A cardboard box is significant in the action.
2   The play starts with 'Goodbye' and ends with 'Hello'. It is set in a car park.
3   The play starts with the sound of a toilet being flushed and ends with the sound of a dog barking.

4   The play starts with someone dancing and ends with someone crying.

5   The play starts with the words 'I don't understand' and ends with the words 'I still don't understand'.

LANGUAGE AND IMAGERY

I asked a friend of mine, who is an actor, what he looks for when he is handed a new play to read. Firstly, he said, he would look for a consciousness of the poetic and a feeling of command in the use of the language; real value being given to the words and how they were used, how the sentences held together. After that, if there were good, dramatic characters or an interesting story. But he was adamant that the use of language came first: 'if you have dull sentence-work and lifeless imagery, then all you have is character and story.' This should be of great interest to us, as writers, for we are creating work for strangers to read, recite or speak. What right have we to offer it to them if it does not give them an experience of language newly made?

I had been working with a group of people in London, all new to writing for live performance. One of them was a young man from Albania, who had found his way to the sessions in the hope that they would help him with his English. At first, when he produced work, he apologised for the fact that it was not 'correct English', but such was the power of how he *used* the language that I – and the rest of the group – said that he had nothing to apologise for. Yes, we said, he did need to learn the correct forms, the grammar, etc. (and we helped him with such things); but he must not lose the instinctive, poetic use of the language he had now. By the end of the project, the group had all contributed to a script, based upon their individual writings. Here is an excerpt from his part of the script:

> My life was in my way. This love was inside me. Suddenly it fell out of my soul. I felt empty, cold and sadness. Huge icy building of loneliness built up surround me. They pour out hate and anger. In a sphere, squashed in two poles, who keep the known space in the limitless universe, the shout of a black cat, germinates the deadly spirits, black maturity of hunger. They are thirsty and they are hungry, I am covered with salt tears. They overload up in my eyelashes and break them. Something is slaughtering inside me. My soul is bowling. O God please help her, us, me to dissolve this disgrace. Here, here, thirsty spirits, here drink my blood, inject the poison into my veins, let it be the last thirst. Here, here, eat my lungs, rip my chest, let it be the last hunger.

I showed this to my friend the actor. 'Exactly', he said.

Writing is a craft – and the craft of writing in play-form is particularly exacting. In this opening chapter we have begun to research some of the basic aspects of the craft. In the following chapters we will dig deeper. Knowledge and understanding of structure, character-development, plot, etc. are basic (whether we are making a five-minute sketch or a three-act tragedy), but what is crucial is what the young man from Albania showed us: the courage and the determination to forge new meanings from the language we are working with.

2   Theme

The *subject matter* of a play can be described in terms of its action: 'two young people in Verona defy their families and bring about their own deaths' (Romeo and Juliet). The *theme* or *themes* are described in more abstract terms and deal with large universal concerns regarding our humanity: love, revenge, duty, tribal loyalties, etc. (Romeo and Juliet). They can also be contained in a large moral or social question, placed firmly at the heart of the narrative: What occurs when we place narrow family duty above the general health of the community? (Romeo and Juliet).

The themes of a play are not necessarily spelled out in an explicit way, but are rather woven into the texture. Hamlet is a complex play not because its subject matter is complicated; indeed, that can be expressed quite simply as, for example, 'by failing to take revenge on his father's murder, a young prince brings death and destruction to the whole court.' The complexity of the play lies in the fact that its themes are so many and so dense: the question of free will, the nature of madness, the limits of the individual, etc. We can say what Hamlet is 'about' in terms of its story, but to finally pin down what it is 'about' in terms of its themes is not so easy.

This principle applies to all texts for performance. I once wrote a large-scale community play for a company in the UK, which dealt with the history of a well-known and derelict stately home (in which the first performance of *A Midsummer Night's Dream* had been given). Local myth and legend, Queen Elizabeth I and a twentieth-century family featured in a travelling performance around the grounds. As we developed the story, it became clear that underneath the subject matter of historical and contemporary events, the strong thematic question of 'who owns history?' was developing. On another occasion, when I was working with primary school children on their own epic tale about tribal conflict, the big question that began to emerge was 'when does group loyalty turn into inter-group conflict?'

Theme is what the story is *really* 'about', and I will be returning to it in more detail in Chapter 8. But, for anyone – groups or individuals – it is important at the early stages to begin to engage with it. However, as with everything else concerning the craft of writing for performance, the themes do not 'just happen'. While you are creating the skeleton of the story and fleshing it out with the actions of your characters, you will probably not be thinking about the big ideas at the heart of the play. That is probably all to the good for, as the American playwright Sam Shepherd has said, 'a play produces ideas, ideas do not produce a play.' When you have your story and your characters, it will be time to see what ideas you have – perhaps unconsciously – been exploring. For the moment, though, let us take a look at how theme or themes are implanted in fully formed plays from the very start.

SETTING THE AGENDA

Exposition at the head of the play alerts the audience as to what to expect in terms of story. Similarly, from the outset the themes of the play are suggested, hinted at and alluded to. You are setting the agenda for what is to come.

Exercise 42 Opening scenes and theme
Part one
Participant: All groups, individual

1   Take an opening scene from a major classic or modern play.

2   Read it through, looking for key words or expressions. Pay no attention to story or character, just focus on the words. There is no 'right or wrong' here; you are looking for those words which seem to you to be of significance.

3   Write down all the words in a list, or if you are working from a photocopy of the text, circle them. Some of the words may occur several times. Make sure to write them out each time. (See Examples 42.1 and 42.2.)

4   You will find that there are groups of words that seem to belong together, in terms of issue, topic, etc. Regroup the words in categories. Again, there is no right or wrong here, just your own individual intuition. If you are working in a group it is interesting to compare

lists and see where individual thoughts on the subject have diverged or coincided. (See Examples 42.3 and 42.4.)

5   On the basis of the above, identify what major themes are suggested in the scene. (See Examples 42.5 and 42.6.)

Example 42.1 *The Seagull*, by Anton Chekhov

Black, unhappy, mourning, life, health, father, rich, comfortably off, life, roubles, superannuation, deducted, mourning, money, pauper, happy, mother, sisters, brother, salary, roubles, eat, drink, tea, sugar, tobacco, scrape, save, act, play, love, souls, create, art, soul, love, longing, nothing, indifference, money, family, marry, touched, love, snuff, thunderstorm, philosophising, money, misfortune, rags, beggar.

Example 42.2 *The Importance of Being Earnest*, by Oscar Wilde

Playing, sir, play, play, play, expression, piano, science, life, sir, science, life, cucumber sandwiches, Lady, sir, Lord, Mr, dining, sir, bottles, champagne, consumed, bottles, pint, bachelor's establishment, servants, drink, champagne, quality, wine, married households, champagne, first-rate, marriage, demoralising, married, family life.

Example 42.3 *The Seagull*

- Black, unhappy, mourning, mourning, nothing, indifference, thunderstorm, misfortune.
- Life, health, life, happy, act, play, create, art.
- Father, mother, sisters, brother, family.
- Rich, comfortably off, roubles, superannuation, deducted, money, pauper, salary, roubles, scrape, save, money, money, rags, beggar.
- Eat, drink, tea, sugar, tobacco, snuff.
- Love, souls, soul, love, longing, marry, touched, love.
- Philosophising.

Example 42.4 *The Importance of Being Earnest*

- Playing, play, play, play, expression, piano.
- Sir, sir, Lady, sir, Lord, Mr, sir, servants.
- Science, life, science, life.

- Cucumber sandwiches, dining, bottles, champagne, consumed, bottles, pint, drink, champagne, wine, champagne.
- Bachelor's establishment, married households, marriage, married, family life.
- Quality, first-rate, demoralising.

Example 42.5 *The Seagull*

On the basis of the evidence provided, we might say that four major themes suggested are Death, Money, Love and Art.

Example 42.6 *The Importance of Being Earnest*

On the basis of the evidence provided, we might say that three major themes suggested are Social Rank, Marriage and Consumption.

Outcome

With all the examples, the writer has peppered the text with words and categories of words that express big, general themes in the plays. They are not spelled out for us, but just as exposition is crafted into the action, so are the themes embedded in the dialogue of the opening scene. We can view this as the writer 'setting the agenda' for what is to proceed. Every writer will approach this differently, but it is useful to apply this general principle to your own work.

Part two – following the themes

Take any of the lists from my examples. Write a dialogue for two or three people. The words in the list must occur in the dialogue, in exactly the order they appear on the page.

'Theme' is the soil in which the narrative is rooted. 'Subject matter' is the narrative fleshed out in action. 'Issue' is the territory that links them: at its most basic, 'a topic of interest or discussion'. In the next chapter we will look at how issue and theme impact on each other in the creation of a narrative for performance.

3   Issue

Theatre that tackles specific contemporary social or political issues – with the aim of leading to or encouraging some type of change – has very deep roots around the world. It takes many forms and is found in many contexts. In India I have seen companies of actors working in the *bastis* (shanty towns), playing to hundreds of people and raising questions about matters that directly relate to the lives of their audience: the inequality of women, government corruption, public transport, etc. Forum Theatre, pioneered by Augusto Boal in Brazil, invites members of the audience to participate in the onstage action and affect the outcome of the debate. It has been used as a vehicle for change in struggles taking place in factories, communities and even in the Brazilian government. So it is always worth remembering that 'theatre' and 'plays' do not necessarily have their home in comfortable arts-centres, and have always had a historical connection with social and political struggles. The movements in theatre that have been conscious of the educational aspect of the work may often be invisible or unrecorded, but they hold a central place in our craft. In the UK in the past decades, groups of people and individual writers made theatre that addressed their own concerns, thus making them the concerns of the wider population: ex-offenders talking about prison conditions and the failings of the justice system, homeless people demonstrating that they are more than a label, black and Asian artists creating their own narratives and styles of work. All taking, to different degrees, an 'issue' which needs public airing through the imaginative capacities of performance.

In the 1970s in the UK a form of theatre was pioneered that placed work in the educational context: Theatre-in-Education (TIE). The plays were very often 'single-issue', raising questions in an informative and provocative way, and were preceded or followed by interactive workshops. Areas of immediate concern, often difficult for the teacher to address directly in the classroom, were expressed in a robust, dramatic form: race-relations, bullying, sexuality, drugs, AIDS, etc. Early TIE plays tended to be collectively devised and to place slightly more emphasis on 'message' as opposed to complex story and character-psychology. As the movement developed, it created its own generations of writers, and it is now regarded not just as 'the place to start' but as a territory of work where some of the best and most rewarding theatre can be found. Someone once said to me, 'but don't you find the "issue" aspect a bit constraining?' My answer was that Henrik Ibsen didn't find the issue of local-government corruption constraining, nor Bernard Shaw the issue of arms manufacturing, nor James Baldwin the issue of racism.

In this chapter we will look at a couple of 'issue-based' projects, and how – while addressing the question-in-hand – they can imaginatively transform what might seem, at the outset, a dry subject into a full theatrical performance.

TACKLING THE ISSUE

In the following work we will look at how a seemingly *most* limiting learning-area can be the stimulus for an original work for performance in the educational context. You can use it in a number of ways:

- As a stimulus for writing a play of your own.
- As a stimulus for writing a play as a group, e.g., your class.
- As a model for a workshop process.

THE TRANSPORT PROJECT

Exercise 43 The context of the project
Participants: All groups, individual

First, we will need to enter into a couple of fictions.

Fiction 1. The commission

You have been commissioned by a theatre company to write a play to go into schools. Here is your brief:

- The play will be for 11–13-year-olds.
- It will be class-length time: 50–55 minutes.
- You can have three actors.
- The play will place young people and their concerns at the heart of the narrative.
- Local schools have come on board as part of your research and development process. They would like the pupils who will see the

play to be involved in the process of story development. You will spend time in the school, working with the pupils and the teacher around (a) the research areas related to the subject matter of the play and (b) story-ideas that come out of this process.

· The schools are this year engaged in projects around the topic of 'Transport'.

· Funding for the tour has been raised on the basis that the play – and the research and development process – will feed into the projects on transport.

· You have a free hand to decide which area of the topic you wish to look at, and to include that in the research and development process.

Fiction 2. The bicycle

· You have chosen the bicycle as the form of transport to consider. You have done this because the play will place at least one young character at the heart of the story. Although many of the pupils may not have a bicycle, it is the one form of transportation that the age group can theoretically have control of. It is also easier to get a working bicycle into a school hall than a working car or aeroplane.

· You will devise research exercises to take into school. They should be designed to (a) stimulate as wide learning-areas as possible and (b) begin to suggest possible storylines.

Exercise 44 About the bicycle

1   Write a list of all the materials that go into making a bicycle. (See Examples 44.1.)

2   Write a list of where those materials might come from. (See Examples 44.2.)

3   Write a list of what sort of people might be involved in obtaining or manufacturing and manufacturing of the materials. What might their status in society be? What might they earn? What might their working conditions be like? (See Examples 44.3.)

Examples 44.1

Steel, rubber, leather, plastic, oil, etc.

Examples 44.2

Rubber from Malaysia, oil from the Middle East, leather from English cattle, etc.

Examples 44.3

The Malaysian rubber-plantation worker: low pay, low status, no employment protection. The steel worker in a factory: decent working person, regular work, but threatened by closure of plant. The boss of an oil company: high social status, very fat salary, but worried about a drop in profits, etc.

Exercise 45 Bicycle images

Write down – or collect – as many images of bicycles as you can. Think of the modern world, think of history, think global. Think of the uses of bicycles.

Examples 45.1

The Grand Prix. A tandem. A penny-farthing. Chinese workers cycling to work en-masse. The mountain bicycle. Refugees with their belongings piled on bicycles, etc.

Exercise 46 The bicycle as symbol

The key parts of the bicycle are the wheels. Wheels are circular. Write down as many things that come to mind when we say 'circle' or 'circular': words, images, phrases, cultural symbols, social events, mythology, etc.

Examples 46.1

The moon, the sun, the seasons, a merry-go-round, 'what goes around comes around', circus rings, wedding rings, curtain rings, circle dancing, the wheel of fortune, etc.

Exercise 47 Problems with bicycles

Write down a list of things that can go wrong with a bicycle.

Examples 47.1

The brakes fail. The tyre bursts. The wheel buckles, etc.

Outcome

In the (fictional) workshops in schools you have now used the humble bicycle to open a window on most of the subject matters on the curriculum: history, geography, economics, social structures, mythology, etc. You have also gathered a wealth of raw material from which to begin to create a narrative.

Exercise 48 Bicycle and story

Using all the above research, write down story-ideas in which a bicycle and a young person are central to what happens. Don't worry if you can't work out the details, or if an ending does not suggest itself. Try and go for the main conflict and make the bicycle central to this. Some will be quite substantial, others can be just a few lines.

Example 48.1

This is an actual story-idea that came out of the workshop I have outlined above. I was working in Singapore with a group of writers, some of whom wanted to write plays for schools. When we came to the exercise on images of bicycles, the subject of the Second World War came up. When Singapore (a British colony at the time) was threatened with invasion by Japan, the British assumed that the attack would come from the sea, along the south of the island. All defences were trained in that direction. In fact, the Japanese arrived in Singapore from the north, having travelled down through Malaysia. Many of the Japanese troops were on bicycles. One writer decided to create a story involving a young Japanese soldier and a twelve-year-old Malaysian boy. The soldier's bicycle has broken down and he is stranded. There is a village nearby, but it is deserted, the villagers having fled, fearing the notoriously cruel soldiers. Only the boy remains. He is an orphan. The boy's dream is to go to England, where they have 'seasons' (unlike Malaysia where the climate is the same all the year round). He has learned this from a British missionary (Malaysia was a British colony also). He also knows by heart Wordsworth's poem about daffodils. The soldier knows the poem too, having studied literature at university. The soldier's dream is to be a poet. They learn all this about each other as the boy helps the soldier mend the bicycle. It transpires that the soldier did not want to go to war, but has never spoken to anyone about this before. The boy decides that, after the war, he and the soldier will go to England together. The soldier becomes anxious that the villagers will return and take revenge. The boy seems to be deliberately slowing down the mending process. He wants the soldier to hide in the village till the war is over. Time is running out and the soldier becomes angry with the boy . . . .

Outcome

In the above example the broken bicycle is the catalyst for the brief friendship between the soldier and the boy, and is a metaphor for dreams that will be broken. 'Journeying' is a theme that is suggested – through life, in war, in the imagination. The play (if it were fully developed and written) would contain historical detail and raise questions about war. It would deal with racial stereotyping (a Japanese soldier who does not want to fight, and a Malaysian village boy who quotes English poetry). It would raise the question of which of the two is more important, practical skills (mending bicycles) or creativity (poetry).

Exercise 49 More issues

Use the model, or variants of it, to explore other issues or topics. For instance, drugs, AIDS, an aspect of local history, the fishing industry, bullying, etc. As with the story-idea in the above example, the aspiration should be to create a complex and fresh story, not a three-dimensional pamphlet.

THE HEALTH PROJECT

The following work can be used as a model for a large-scale community play.

Exercise 50 The context of the project
Participants: All groups

Once again, we will start by entering into some fictions.

Fiction 1. The community play

You have been employed by a local authority to produce a large-scale community play that addresses the following question: What creates a healthy community?

Fiction 2. The community

You will be working with a broad, representative range of people from the area – health workers, residents, teachers, community workers, students, etc. – to research and develop the ideas. There will be a mix of age, physical ability, class, ethnicity, etc.

Fiction 3. The process

The ideas and some of the text will come from a development process taking place over a weekend. You will be working with a team that includes a director, a movement-artist, a designer and a musician. Your responsibility will be to lead the work that produces the ideas and some of the text. After this you will refine and shape the text into a narrative.

Exercise 51 Getting going

Many of the people you are working with will not have written in this context before. Select some of the 'Getting going' exercises from Chapter 1. If it helps, you can adapt the exercises to suit the subject matter of the project: 'Health' and 'Community'. (See Examples 51.1 and 51.2.)

Example 51.1 Community

From Chapter 1, take Exercises 3 (Parts 1–3). This will help create a level playing field of shared experience/memory for the participants, and also focus the work on the area they live in.

Example 51.2 Health

Write a list of 20–25 words, then choose ones that – directly or indirectly – relate to 'health' (or its opposite) in some way. For instance, Nurse, Bed, Air, Confidence, Sky, Smile, Cigarette, Trust, etc.

Exercise 52 The universal needs

1 Working individually, write out as long a list as you can of those things you consider to be *universally necessary to sustain life*. (See Examples 52.1.)

2 In small groups, compare lists. Remember that we are looking for those things that are *universal* and *necessary* to sustain life. Draw circles around those words that do not fit these definitions. (See Examples 52.2.)

3 In the small groups, look at all the words on the lists that have not been circled. Identify 10–12 things you consider *absolutely universal* and *absolutely necessary* to sustain life. Write each word on a sheet of A4 paper, in large capitals, with a felt marker. (See Examples 52.3.)

4   Each small group will now have 10–12 sheets of A4 with key words on them. The next step is to make a map of them on the floor. The map will be made up of clusters of words that stand for the same thing. This does not have to be rushed. One person will begin the process, then a second will add their word and so on. (See Examples 52.4.) The layout of the map can be renegotiated a couple of times. The aim is to agree, as a whole group, on the final list of universal needs. Write out the final list. (See Examples 52.5.)

Examples 52.1

Love, Food, Water, Warmth, Communication, Creativity, Touch, Light, Shelter, Oxygen, Spirituality, Space, Greenery, Self-expression, Movement, Other people, Privacy, Reflectivity, Money, Hope, Dreams, Curiosity, Desire, Health, Laughter, Sex, Education, Stimulation, Name, Identity, Self-worth, Music, etc.

Examples 52.2

- *Other people*: in all ages there have been people who have withdrawn totally from social existence.

- *Greenery*: some cultures exist in regions where there is no greenery.

- *Privacy*: in some cultures the Western notion of 'privacy' has no meaning; life still goes on in crowded prisons.

- Etc.

Examples 52.3

Food. Water. Light. Shelter. Oxygen. Spirituality. Movement. Hope. Stimulation. Identity.

Examples 52.4

A map, with everyone's contributions, could look like this:

Food.	Oxygen.	Protection.
Water. Sustenance.	Air. Light.	Shelter. Warmth.
		Rest.

Communication.	Space.
Education. Love.	Privacy. Self-expression.
Movement.	Identity.

| Spirituality.   Creativity. |
| The Transcendental.   Dreams. Hope. |
| Stimulation. |

Examples 52.5

A final list might be: Sustenance, Air, Light, Rest, Creativity, Identity, The Transcendental, Love, Connection, Shelter, Creativity.

Outcome

We have defined 'Health' as based upon needs that are not related simply to the material. The creative and the spiritual are as necessary as the need for food and shelter. The piece of work addressing the question 'How do we create a healthy community?' will explore the full range of needs.

Exercise 53 Satisfying the needs

1   Identify for each need (a) what might be a true satisfier and (b) what might be a false satisfier. (See Examples 53.1.)

2   Identify where and how these needs (true and false) are provided for (or not) in the area or community. (See Examples 53.2.)

3   This step uses Exercise 22 in Chapter 2. Work in small groups. Think about the area you live in. Think of a type of person who might be living in the community. Create a thumbnail sketch of the person.

4   Decide how they have spent their day. Write down (a) three needs that were truly satisfied on that day, and (b) three needs that were falsely satisfied on that day. (See Example 53.3.)

Examples 53.1

•   *Sustenance*: water (true), coke (false).

•   *Air*: unpolluted (true), air conditioning (false).

•   *Light*: natural (true), neon strip lighting (false).

•   *Rest*: siesta (true), sleeping pills (false).

•   *Creativity*: making your own dance (true), copying a pop star's movements (false).

•   *Identity*: speaking your mind (true), saying what you think pleases people (false).

•   Etc.

Examples 53.2

•   Local shops stock mineral water, but the schools have coke-vending machines.

- There is a hill that gets a fresh breeze, but it is surrounded on three sides by a motorway.
- There are no tall buildings, so the sun gets everywhere, but the street lighting at night blocks the view of the stars.
- There are some creative evening classes on offer, but they are more expensive than hiring a video for the night.
- Etc.

Example 53.3

- She worked all day in an office with strip lighting and air conditioning. During the course of the day she drank three cans of coke.
- In the evening she went to a modern dance class. In the pub afterwards she drank mineral water. When someone made a racist remark she challenged the speaker.

Outcome

We have now begun to identify (a) aspects of 'health' that are specific to the local community, and (b) possible characters within the community and how they satisfy their basic needs. In both cases there are interesting contradictions and paradoxes. You now have the basis of a narrative that will address the practical issues at the core of the project, within the frame of a strong, dramatic set of situations.

We shall now look at another technique for opening up an area of debate/discussion to see what its thematic potential is.

ISSUE INTO THEME

When faced with an 'issue' to be discussed (whether in the classroom, round the dinner table or in a writing group) there is a tendency to launch into opinions. If these opinions are backed up by facts, they will shed light on the subject under discussion. However, if we wish to make a piece of work that not only serves its subject matter, but is also a satisfying and complex drama, we must strive to go beyond the surface issue and seek the deeper themes. The first exercises in this chapter have provided models for how this may be achieved. This one approaches the same task of converting issue into theme by using a technique that appears throughout the book: asking questions that lead to other questions.

Exercise 54 Questions leading to questions

Participants: All groups, individual

1   Take a specific issue: one that addresses a major social concern. (See Examples 54.1.)

2   Working individually, write down three questions that the issue raises in your mind. They may be very direct questions necessitating further information, or they may be rhetorical questions. (See Examples 54.2.)

3   For each question in step 2, write down three questions that are prompted by them. You will now have nine new questions. (See Examples 54.3.)

4   For each question in step 3, write down three questions that are prompted by them. The questions may become very personal to you, and they may not seem to be addressing the core of the issue. That is a good thing. Trust your intuition and remember all the time that you are not seeking answers, but spreading the net of questions as wide as you can. You will now have 27 new questions. (See Example 54.4.)

5   Write each question on a sheet of paper. Make a map of them on the floor or on a wall. What cluster-groups of question emerge? What broad, general themes are suggested?

6   From all the cluster-groups, frame three or four broad questions concerning 'the rights of children' that might suggest (a) possible narratives and (b) universal themes.

Examples 54.1

The rights of young people.

·   Live animals and scientific research.

·   The fashion industry and sweatshop labour.

Examples 54.2

The rights of young people.

·   Do young people have rights?

·   What is a right?

·   What is 'young'?

Examples 54.3

Do young people have rights?

- Should young people have rights?
- Do young people have duties?
- Do young people care if they have rights?

What is a right?

- Who decides what rights we have?
- How do I know what rights I have?
- Can I decide what I want to do?

What is 'young'?

- Is being young better than being old?
- Why are young people seen as a problem?
- What do we mean by 'youth culture'?

Example 54.4

Should young people have rights?

- What makes you happy?
- Do I have the right to be happy?
- How much money should young people have?

Do young people have duties?

- [Your own example]
- [Your own example]
- [Your own example]

Do young people care if they have rights?

- [Your own example]
- [Your own example]
- [Your own example]
- Etc.

Outcome

- By constantly broadening the scope of enquiry, we have begun to discover that a one-issue subject matter contains a multitude of possible themes: happiness, age, culture, power, duty, knowledge, etc.

By framing the enquiry through questions and avoiding opinion, we have not foreclosed on the subject matter.

• This approach is particularly useful in large groups, where a range of opinions may exist, and which need to be accommodated, explored and even challenged. Questions often reveal far more about real feelings and attitudes than instant reflexive answers and solutions.

In Chapters 2 and 3, we have begun to explore how whole narratives may evolve, both group-written and individually composed. We have referred back to some of the exercises in Chapter 1 as part of this process. In the following chapters we will look in more detail at the way a whole text for performance can be created, and some of the universal underlying principles of dramatic narrative for performance.

4 Building a character

In Chapter 1 we looked at ways in which fictional characters can be developed from material that is instantly available to us in daily life. We began to look at the components of what we mean by 'character': inner- and outer-life, personal history, characteristics, etc. Now we will create a fully rounded character, whose story will contain the seeds of a full dramatic narrative.

All of the exercises in this chapter can be used by the individual writer, or provide the basis for work in a group workshop.

BEING SPECIFIC ABOUT THE CHARACTER

We will begin by looking at some fully developed plays, to see how the writers have approached the task of revealing 'characters' to us. For my examples I have chosen *The Seagull*, by Anton Chekhov, and *Death of a Salesman*, by Arthur Miller. In your own use of this exercise, any major play from any cultural origin could work equally well.

Exercise 55 Facts about the character
Participants: All groups, individual

1   Take an opening scene from a couple of major plays.

2   Choose one of the main characters in the scene.

3   Go through the text carefully and write down the *things we know* about the character, on the basis of: (a) what character X says about her/himself and (b) what the other characters say about character X. (See Examples 55.1–55.4.)

4   Be specific. Write down the evidence from what you are given in the text. We are seeking the facts the playwright has given us, not our own opinions or speculations on what the character 'might be like'.

Example 55.1 *The Seagull*. What Masha says about herself

In the opening moments of *The Seagull*, there is a conversation between Medvedenko (a teacher) and a young woman called Masha. Let us see what she reveals to us about herself in this exchange.

* She is in mourning for her life.
* She thinks even a beggar can be happy.
* She's very touched that Medvedenko loves her.
* She can't return Medvedenko's love.
* She takes snuff.

Example 55.2 *The Seagull*. What Medvedenko says about Masha

* She always wears black.
* Her father is not rich, but he's not badly off.
* Her soul has no point of contact with Medvedenko.
* She shows indifference to Medvedenko, though he walks three miles daily to see her.

Example 55.3 *Death of a Salesman*. What Willy says about himself

In the opening exchange of *The Death of a Salesman*, Willy Loman (a travelling salesman) returns home early from a job. He is talking to his wife, Linda. These are the things he reveals about himself in the exchange.

* He's tired to death.
* He couldn't make it [the long drive to work].
* He suddenly couldn't drive any more.
* His arch-supports are killing him.
* He has strange thoughts.
* He's a New England man, not a New York man [in his work].
* He's supposed to see his employers the next morning.
* He's worked a lifetime to pay off the house.
* He didn't lose his temper with his son that morning.

- He doesn't remember if he apologised to his son before he left.
- He thinks that his son is wasting his life.
- He thinks his son is lazy.
- He wants to know why his son came back home to live.
- He intends to persuade his son to become a salesman.
- He prefers Swiss cheese to American cheese.
- He's always being contradicted.
- He and his son had once hung a swing in the garden.
- He constantly remembers the days when they had a proper garden.
- He thinks the population is out of control.
- His foundation and support is Linda.
- He won't fight with his son anymore.
- He believes in his son.
- In 1928 he had a red Chevy [car].

Example 55.4 *Death of a Salesman*. What Linda tells us about Willy

- He looks terrible.
- He never went for his new glasses.
- He can't carry on as he is.
- His mind is overactive.
- There's no reason why he can't work in New York.
- He's sixty years old.
- He's too accommodating.
- He lost his temper with his son that morning.
- His son admires him.

Outcome

From the above examples we have identified a range of detailed 'facts' about the characters:

- What they wear (black clothes; arch-supports).
- What they have a liking for (snuff; Swiss cheese).
- What their economic circumstances are (daughter of a not-badly off father; struggling salesman).

- What their inner lives are like (in mourning for her life; having strange thoughts).

- What their personal relationships contain (indifference towards an admirer; concern for a son).

Some of these 'facts' include opinions and beliefs the characters hold (or, for the moment, seem to hold), memories they retain, etc. They also begin to give us a sense of people with *contradictions*: Masha allows Medvedenko to see her daily, yet is indifferent to him; Willy claims he didn't lose his temper with his son, but Linda says he did. All these things may seem placed in the text at random, but they are not. They are things that the writer has deliberately *chosen*, to give us a sense of unique and complex individuals. Masha is not just *any* young woman who is indifferent to the attentions of a young man: she is the one who takes snuff and always wears black. Willy is not just *any* tired travelling salesman having worries about his son: he is the one who wears arch-supports and drove a red Chevvy in 1928.

What Chekhov and Miller are both aiming at is specificity of detail, and that is your task when building all the characters inhabiting the play you are writing. The specificity may be in 'big things' of the soul or the psyche (Masha in mourning for her life, Willy in having 'strange thoughts'), but it also resides in small and daily things (snuff and shoe-arches).

Both of these plays are in the naturalistic mould: human beings in recognisable social environments, struggling with their situation and their emotions. What about more abstract plays, where we are not given similar frames of reference? Does the principle of revealing the characters through what they say/what is said about them still apply?

Exercise 56 More facts about the character

Participants: All groups, individual

Take a play that is more abstract in form, in which the characters do not seem as 'nailed down' in terms of social status, economic situation, emotional state, etc. I have used *Waiting for Godot*, by Samuel Beckett, but any text that is non-naturalistic will do. Apply the same method. What hard facts about the character does the text reveal?

Example 56.1 *Waiting for Godot*. What Estragon says about himself

At the start of *Waiting for Godot*, we meet two men on a country road. Estragon is sitting on a mound. Vladimir enters. The action of the opening passage involves Estragon attempting to get his boot off. There is nothing about the pair or their surroundings that gives us clues as to who they are or what their situation is. These are the things we learn from Estragon about himself:

- He spent last night in a ditch.
- They beat him.
- He doesn't know if it was the same lot [who beat him].
- The boot he is struggling with hurts.

Example 56.2 *Waiting for Godot*. What Vladimir says about Estragon

- Without Vladimir, he would be nothing more than a little heap of bones.
- He used to be respectable.
- He wouldn't be let up the Eiffel Tower.
- He thinks he's the only one who suffers.
- He doesn't listen to Vladimir.
- He thinks he's the only one who ever suffers.
- He doesn't have the thing that hurts Vladimir.

Example 56.3 *Waiting for Godot*. What Vladimir says about himself

- He's beginning to come around to the opinion that there's 'nothing to be done'.
- He's tried all his life to put the opinion 'from him' [ignore it].
- He 'resumed the struggle' [with the opinion].
- He's pleased to see Estragon.
- He'd thought Estragon had gone forever.
- He doesn't know where Estragon would be without him.
- He believes there's no good in losing heart now.
- He should have had that thought when the world was young, in the nineties [1890s].
- He imagines jumping off the Eiffel tower with Estragon, in the nineties.
- He used to be respectable.
- He wouldn't be allowed up the Eiffel tower these days.
- He believes boots must be taken off every day.

- He's tired.
- He wants to know why Estragon doesn't listen to him.
- He's got something that hurts.
- He believes the little things in life should never be neglected.
- He wants to know who said 'hope deferred maketh the something sick'.
- He doesn't count [in Estragon's eyes] when it comes to suffering.
- He sometimes feels hope coming.
- When he feels hope coming he goes 'all queer' [as in 'odd feeling'].
- The odd feeling he gets is a mixture of being relieved and being appalled.
- He finds the thought 'funny' [odd].

Example 56.4 *Waiting for Godot.* What Estragon says about Vladimir

- He shouldn't be surprised if the thing that he has hurts him.
- He always waits 'till the last moment'.

Outcome

In *The Seagull* and *Death of a Salesman*, even though some of the 'facts' we learn may just be the characters' opinions of themselves and of each other, they are given within a recognisable social and emotional frame. We do not doubt that Willy is a salesman, and it seems probable that Medvedenko is in love with Masha. On a first read, things seem much less substantial with Estragon and Vladimir. There are enigmatic references to being beaten by unknown people, to having once been respectable, and to access to the Eiffel Tower. Estragon seems the easier character to grasp. He probably spent the night in a ditch, possibly got beaten and is fully preoccupied with the boot that hurts. With Vladimir, there seems just to be a lot of random philosophising, particularly around the subject of suffering. In fact, it is exactly here that he is being most concrete for – as we discover – the thing that is hurting him is a painful condition of the bowels. His preoccupation with such matters of 'the little things of life', being 'relieved and appalled', and Estragon's reference to waiting 'till the last moment' are all concerned with bowel movements. Underneath the surface of a scene in which the characters seem hugely enigmatic, we have a situation between two characters that is as specific as the ones in *The Seagull* and *Death of a Salesman*. We have a man who is desperate to get a painful boot off his foot. We have another man who's just come back from his ablutions. That was also clearly painful. They quarrel about who suffers most.

In the case of all three plays, we are learning about the characters in specific and detailed ways without realising it.

Exercise 57 Conjuring up a character
Participants: All groups, individual (3–4 minutes)

Following the examination of how characters can be revealed through detail, you are going to create a fictional character of your own. Here are the rules:

- Go for someone very different from yourself.
- Avoid basing the character on any real person.
- Follow the instructions and don't think too hard.
- You know nothing about this person.

Write down the following.

- Their gender.
- Their age.
- Their ethnicity.
- Their name.
- Three physical characteristics (of appearance, mannerism, tone of voice, etc.).
- Where their money comes from (work or otherwise).
- What sort of accommodation they live in.
- Where exactly on the world map is that accommodation.
- Something they lack in life.
- Something they need right now.
- A secret they have.
- A problem they have.
- A memory they have.
- Something they believe.
- Something they wish for.
- Where they are at this very moment.
- What they are doing at this very moment.
- What they are thinking or saying at this very moment.
- Three other things you know about them having written this list.

Example 57.1

This is how the exercise worked for me.

> Male, 78, Asian. Taresh. He walks with a limp, smokes a pipe and is bald. He works in a tobacconist's shop. He lives in a small rented attic-room. It is in a side-street in Sheffield in the UK. He lacks friendship. Right now he needs some more tobacco for his pipe. He secretly steals pipe-tobacco when the shop-owner is out. He has a problem with his back. He remembers the time when he lived by a beach. He believes that his landlord is a murderer. He wishes he could live by the beach again. At this moment he is in the shop alone. He is opening the jar with pipe-tobacco in it. He is saying to himself, 'The woman is a miser anyway, if she paid me well I'd not have to be a thief.' He reads comic books, he keeps his money under the mattress, and he goes to the opera once a year.

Outcome

You have now created a character in some detail. The details range from the physical to the emotional; from the daily to the psychological. Contradictions exist within the character. Taresh, the Asian man in the example, could well provide the basis for further development. Someone who justifies petty theft, harbours suspicions about his landlord, longs to live by a beach, and goes to the opera once a year raises many interesting questions.

Exercise 58 Questions about the character
Participants: All groups, individual

Think about the character you created in the last exercise. Prompted by the things you discovered, write down as many questions as possible. Don't try to answer the questions.

Examples 58.1

- How did Taresh get his limp?
- Why does he lack friendship?
- Why does he have a problem with his back?
- When did he live near a beach?
- Where was the beach?
- Why does he wish he still lived near the beach?
- Will he ever get to go back to the beach?

- Why does he think his landlord is a murderer?
- Who is his landlord?
- Does the landlord live in the same building?
- How long has he lived in Sheffield?
- Where in Sheffield does he live?
- How long has he worked in the shop?
- Where in Sheffield is the shop?
- Who is the woman who owns the shop?
- How long has he been stealing the tobacco?
- Why does he keep his money under the mattress?
- How much money has he got under the mattress?
- What sort of comics does he read?
- Why does he read comic books?
- What is his favourite opera?
- What is it he likes about the opera?

Outcome

You have now expanded the range of enquiry into your character. By asking questions (ones to which you don't necessarily know the answers) you have kept your options open. At some point you will begin to select, but not quite yet.

Exercise 59 Answering the questions
Participants: All groups, individual

Answer the questions you asked in Exercise 58.

Exercise 60 Practical research
Participants: All groups, individual

The last exercise may now suggest you do some practical research. There will be aspects of your character's life that may be unfamiliar to you, and so some detailed practical knowledge could shift the development further.

Example 60.1

- Listen to some opera. Find a book of opera-plot-lines.
- Think of all the beaches you have been on. Look at pictures of coast-lines all around the world.
- See if there is a specialist tobacconist's near you – the old-fashioned type that keep the tobacco in jars.
- What is Sheffield like? Is there an Asian community in Sheffield?
- Read a selection of comic books.
- If you don't rent a room from a landlord, find out how it works. What's advertised? What is the price of renting? Look at buildings that are divided into flats.
- Any reports of murderous landlords in your local paper lately?

Outcome

Now you will have gathered further raw material from which to draw. With the example, we could now see Taresh in his current environment and have a range of choices regarding the beach he dreams of. We would have a range of operas and comic books to consider. Murders in seedy attic-rooms suggest themselves.

Exercise 61 What's in a name?
Participants: All groups, individual

Your character has a name. Use Exercise 22 in Chapter 1 to discover what their name reveals about them.

Exercise 62 Murdering babies
Participants: All groups, individual

Through the exercises above, you have created and gathered your raw material. You have a recognisable and distinct character, with thoughts, feelings, flaws and some history. There will be more to come, but now is the time to consider which elements are to be (a) retained, (b) given prominence and (c) abandoned. This is perhaps a good moment to note the following: decisions made now can be reversed later, if that suits your purposes. I don't know why exactly, but I have noted in some writers I have worked with, and myself, that there can be a tendency to hang onto something just because 'it's there'. I know that I have ruined plays of my own by refusing to dispense with a character who I liked, but who was not at all necessary; or a scene that made me chuckle, but which added nothing at all to the dynamic of the plot. So don't be afraid to throw overboard anything which seems untrue or irrelevant at the moment. If they really are necessary, they will find their way back. You will be surprised when a character you scrapped in Draft Two of your play suddenly pops up in Draft Four. A piece of advice I was given once, regarding getting over-fond of passages the play can do without, was 'we have to learn to murder our babies'. Sometimes a character becomes very dear to us; so dear in fact, that even when we know they are not helping the play at all, we can't bear to dismiss them. So, starting from now, see if there are any babies to be killed off.

That said, don't throw the birth certificate out with the baby. Keep all your notes on the character. File the profiles on cards and retain them. The baby may need to be brought back to life at a later date.

Go through the work on your character. Be as rigorous with yourself as possible. Don't hang on to anything if you cannot justify its inclusion.

1   What aspects of the character should be developed?

2   What aspects should be disposed of?

3   Are there any new aspects that suggest themselves?

4   What possibilities for story development are suggested? Explore three or four options. Try different groupings of information about the character. (See Examples 62.1.)

5   Choose one.

Examples 62.1

With Taresh and the possible development of his character, and a story for him, I came up with the following options.

Option (a): Murder (or suspected murder) and petty theft are both on the menu. The murder option is very high-level on the plot-development scale. To go down that route right now might close doors on a more mundane – but possibly more interesting – investigation into the character of Taresh. On the other hand, petty theft from his employer (and possibly the only other person working in the shop, someone who Taresh would have daily contact and a personal relationship with) could throw more light on his character.

Option (b): A 78-year old Asian man who reads comics and goes to the opera once a year marks Taresh out as different from the next 78-year old Asian man. Perhaps an exploration of just one of these personal interests might be enough to give an insight into who Taresh is. I would suggest that the opera-option might give greater scope, given that 'going to the opera' is a social event, while reading comics is a solitary one. Given that a play (even if it is a monologue) is about social interaction of some sort, I would suggest that the opera be given prominence and the comics take a bit of a back-seat as character-detail.

Option (c): Taresh obviously has money problems – lives in a rented accommodation, can't afford to buy the tobacco he sells, seems not to be able to live near the beach he once lived by, goes to the opera only once a year. Yet he has money under the mattress, he buys comics, he does manage to buy an opera ticket once a year. I would suggest that all of this should be retained and developed: the complexities and contradictions of life – in fiction and in reality – are essentially bound up with those of material existence. Refer to previous work in this chapter, where we discovered essential things about Masha and Willy through mention of economic circumstances.

Outcome

In the different options, you have now murdered some babies, promoted some others and relegated some to second rank. Always remember that they might come back, if needed. What you have now is an outline of a believable character in a believable situation. What you need to do now is to give that character a believable past.

Exercise 63 More history for the character
Participants: All groups, individual

Read over everything you have written about your character. Some of the things you have written will give clues to the following questions, and may indeed have answered them. If not, the following may fill in some gaps. Answer the questions, and see if the answers prompt further questions.

1   Where were they born?

2   When were they born?

3   Who were their parents or adult carers?

4   What sort of family life/home life did they have?

5   What sort of education did they have?

6   What was a good early experience they had?

7   What was a bad early experience they had?

8   Who made them what they are?

Example 63.1

- Taresh was born in Bali. (Where is Bali, what is its culture?)
- He was born in 1928. (What was Bali like in 1928?)
- His parents were farmers. (What sort of farming?)
- He had three sisters and three brothers and lots of uncles and aunts. They all lived in the same village. (Who were his favourite relatives? Who were the relatives he did not like?)
- He had no formal education. (How did he learn, and from who?)
- Being taught to sing by his uncle. (What was the song?)
- Being taught to steal by his elder sister. (What did he steal?)
- The old man at the edge of the village. (What did the old man tell him?)

Outcome

You have now given your character an early-life history. Once again, you have raised more questions, which will give rise to even more questions, and possible research.

Exercise 64 Research

Participants: All groups, individual

Research on the questions raised in Exercise 63. The research may be factual (in the example, what was Bali like in 1928, what was the culture there?) or imaginative, but helped by the factual (in the example, what was Taresh's uncle like, what was his sister like?).

Exercise 65 Evidence

Participants: All groups, individual

There might be some other examples of 'evidence' about your character that could be useful in building up the bigger picture. Use any of the following if you find them helpful:

1   Birth certificate.

2   School report.

3   CV.

4   Reference from previous employer.

5   Letter of advice from parent or significant adult.

6   Love letter from admirer.

7   Police report.

8   Obituary in the newspaper.

Outcome

You will now have information about your character that arrives from very different points of view, all giving very differing and interesting perspectives on the individual. Always remember that what the other characters say about character X is as revealing as anything X say about themselves.

Exercise 66 The character's journey
Participants: All groups, individual

Think about the life-story of your character. Chart the progress of the character from their birth up to the present moment – that is, where we meet them at the start of the play. By 'progress' I mean 'journey'. By 'journey' I mean both external and internal: physical journey and emotional journey, economic journey and spiritual journey.

1   Have ten blank postcards. Number them. Number 1 is the start of their journey, number 10 is the moment we meet them in the play.

2   Write on the top of each card a significant *event* in the character's life-journey. By *events* I mean things that were observable and social (left home, won the Oscar, got imprisoned for life, discovered a new planet, etc.

3   Try to keep the events evenly spread out along the course of their life – like items of washing strung out on a line.

4   The washing line image is useful, in that it will have items of different sizes hanging from it. Some of your events will be huge and bed-sheet-sized (death of a loved one) and others the size of a cushion cover (winning a prize at school) or a handkerchief (enjoying a particular film).

5   Under each *event*, write down the answers to the following:

   •   What was the character feeling and thinking at the time?

   •   What were the economic circumstances the character was in at the time?

- Who was the character in contact with at the time?
- What different choices did the character have/not have at the time?
- What choices did the character make/not make at the time?

Example 66.1

- What were the ten key stages of Taresh's life journey from Bali in 1928 to Sheffield in 2003?
- What were his feelings along the way, on all the stages of that journey? How did his thinking develop?
- How did he manage economically along the way?
- Who did he meet along the way and what effect did these meetings have?
- What decisions did he make/not make and how did they affect his journey?

Outcome

You now have a skeleton-of your character's life journey. But remember, it is all in developmental stage and babies can still be murdered.

Exercise 67 Don't forget the other characters
Participants: All groups, individual

Other characters will have begun to emerge. They will also need to be as fully rounded as your major character, and some degree of similar work will have to be put into them. Write thumbnail sketches of all the other characters. With other major characters, you will need to examine them in fuller detail, using methods we have explored.

Exercise 68 The back-story
Participants: All groups, individual

You are soon going to write a full life-history of your character, based upon everything you have done so far; but before that, there are some things I would like you to consider.

What you have begun to do, through these exercises, is to create what film-makers term the 'back-story' of your character(s) – quite literally, 'the story behind the story'. That is, all the elements of the life of the character(s).

It would be worth taking a moment to think about what exactly 'back-story' means, and how it can help us enormously with the character(s) we are creating (and later – as we shall see in Chapter 5 – the development of narrative). I have used the phrase 'raw material' a couple of times, and that is just what it is. If we are going to create characters who are absolutely unique, who are not stereotypes, then we need to know them in all their detail. Already we know that Taresh in the example is not just *any* Asian working in a shop in the UK city of Sheffield. The characters you are building will also emerge as unique in their own rights. So is 'back-story' a random selection of events, memories, feelings, etc.; or can it be seen as a more systematic look at our character? I suggest that when you come to review all the work you have put into developing the character, all of the following categories should have been touched upon:

- The inner world of the character: those things that happen in the heart, the head and the soul. The thoughts, dreams, feelings, ambitions, fears . . . (continue the list).

- The immediate, intimate outer world of the character: the nurturers, the lovers, the friendships, the familial . . . (continue the list).

- The wider social world of the character: the teachers, colleagues, shopkeepers . . . (continue the list).

- The institutional world the character might come into contact with: relations with employers, police, the professions, religious bodies . . . (continue the list).

- The specific places and times that the character inhabits.

Now go back over all the material you have written and researched. Write out the character's back-story, eliminating those things that no longer seem to fit and adding new things as they suggest themselves. Following on from the previous notes, try not to go for just the 'externals' ('she did this and then she did that') but allow the inner life to emerge, explore what the character is thinking and feeling. While you are doing this, keep the following in mind:

- Don't go for the obviously 'dramatic' just for the sake of it. Guns, baby-eating, and grandmothers-under-the floorboards *may* finally be essential to the story, but if they are forced onto the story you could end up with an all-action, no-character melodrama.

- Is what you are inventing true to the nature of your character? People do change, of course – and plays are essentially about watching how people do or do not change – but if your sweet-tempered, humanistic character suddenly becomes a raging fascist we will need to see very clearly how and why that happens. There is a play called *Good* by a writer called C.P. Taylor, in which a humanist university lecturer in Germany in the 1930s eventually becomes a commandant of a concentration camp. As a study of the journey from light to dark in a human soul, and how the dramatist charts that journey, it is well worth a look at. It is an excellent example of a play that asks us what we would do, if we found ourselves in a similar situation: would we take the same path?

• Coincidence does happen in life, but be sparing with it in the life of your character. If a 'good angel' turns up once, when your character is in a spot of trouble, that may be fine; but if they keep turning up whenever there is a difficulty they will lose credibility.

• You may find that you are writing a very fine short story. Good. You may be a fine short-story writer as well as a playwright.

Outcome

You have now created a full world and a full life for your character. Some of these things will be fully in the play, some of them only alluded to. All of them will inform your knowledge of the character and the journey they are on.

Exercise 69 An opening moment or scene
Participants: All groups, individual

1 Choose a moment in the life of your character with which to open the play.

2 Include at least two characters. Don't bring in peripheral characters unless absolutely necessary.

3 Go for something low-key, but with suggestions and hints of conflicts and tensions beneath the surface. Think of Masha's indifference to her suitor, and Willy's concern about his son.

4 Bring something in to mark it as different from all the other days – on this day, Medvedenko, the daily suitor, asks Masha why she always wears black; on this day Willy fails to make the work-journey.

5 Try for a scene of some length, 200–300 words. Don't worry if it doesn't complete itself, focus on getting the characters talking.

Example 69.1

I would suggest that we first encounter Taresh in the tobacconist's shop. My advice would be to keep it quite 'daily'. Petty theft may happen, but for the moment, hold off. Allow us to observe the routine of the place, establish the status of the characters (employer–employee) and the temperature of their relationship; then bring in some element that marks this day out as different from any other – Taresh raising the question of how much he is paid, perhaps. How and how many times does he do it? How does the employer respond, or not respond? Bring in those things from the back-story which are useful at this point. Don't overload the audience with information. Don't be afraid of what might *seem* undramatic. If the characters have intentions or needs, those things will inform what is going on. Remember Masha and Willy. Masha refuses to engage with Medvedenko, Willy wants to sort his son out. Both those drives take place in relatively low-key dramatic moments: there are no guns, baby-eating or grannies-under-the-floorboards.

Outcome

You will now have created an opening moment for your play, in which you will have begun to reveal your character or characters. That is *they are ready to be set in motion*. Of course, they are already alive and active and some of their inner contradictions and outer problems have been revealed; but in terms of a dramatic narrative nothing much has happened. As we shall see, real 'character' is only revealed when the individual is put under pressure; that is, when events conspire to force them to make *choices*.

SETTING THE CHARACTERS IN MOTION

In the previous exercises you created a character with a rich history, alongside other characters with their own individuality. Conflicts (social, personal, moral, etc.) and key events were referred to or suggested. You also created an opening scene that introduced two of the characters. Before we proceed, you may need to do some more work on that scene.

Exercise 70 Rewriting the opening scene
Participants: All groups, individual

Look at your opening scene. Ask yourself the following questions and see if they prompt you to sharpen the scene up a little.

1   Does it contain a dilemma, a source of tension, a hint of things to come for the character(s)?

2   Does it give a sense of the intentions or 'wants' or 'needs' (conscious or unconscious) of the character(s)?

3   Does it give rise to (perhaps subconscious) questions in the mind of the audience?

4   Rewrite the scene.

Examples 70.1

*   Willy's frustration with his own life is compounded by his frustration with his son.

*   Willy wants to put his son's life straight.

*   Willy needs to put his own life straight.

*   Will the conflict around the son's life be resolved? Will he turn his own life round?

Outcome

Any opening scene will contain some of these – or similar – elements. You have now begun to ask yourself 'what do the characters' *want?* When we have discovered what their real wants, needs and desires are, we will begin to know what their real *drives* are. And then we will have *fully* set them in motion.

Exercise 71 The drives of the character

Participants: All groups, individual

You will soon be looking at (a) how you set your character(s) *fully* in motion and (b) what their *drives* really are. Before that, there are some points we need to consider. Some of them will be familiar, but they are worth going over again. I am going to illustrate them by referring to two example-narratives: Macbeth and Little Red Riding Hood.

Example 71.1 *Macbeth*

As a general principle, nothing very much happens when we first meet our main character(s). Potential sources of dramatic conflict may be suggested, outlines of future problems may be raised, and questions left unanswered may be posed. We do not even have to meet our main character(s) in the first scene: Macbeth does not appear until Scene 3, Act 1. But the point is that (as a general principle) we encounter the main character(s) in quite an ordinary way. By 'ordinary', I mean ordinary in terms of the world they live in. In Macbeth's world, the ordinary is that of feudal loyalties and terrible battles (just as in Willy's it is of the daily slog-to-work of the travelling salesman). All of this is part of the *exposition*, which we will be looking at in more detail later on.

As a general principle, the *function* of the first encounter with our main character(s) is to:

- Allow us to observe the *status quo*: the life of the characters as it generally is, the way they are regarded or regard themselves and the others around them. Feudal duties as a loyal general (Macbeth), or the daily slog-to-work as a faithful employee (Willy). That is who they are, that is what they do, and that is how they go about it.

- Indicate to us that this particular day is marked out as slightly – or even more than slightly – different from all the others; although not so different as to change the status quo. Let us see what happens when we first meet Macbeth. He has already been set up as a good and loyal servant of the king; 'brave Macbeth – well he deserves that name'; 'O valiant cousin! Worthy gentleman!'; 'noble Macbeth'. In the next scene, Macbeth is riding back from battle, which we assume is his version of 'the daily routine', when he meets three witches who tell him that (a) he'll soon be thane of Cawdor and (b) after that he'll get to be king. Macbeth is a bit puzzled by all this and asks them how they know all these things, but they disappear without letting on. Very quickly someone else arrives from the king, saying that the traitorous thane of Cawdor has been executed and that he – Macbeth – has been given the title. This is big news for Macbeth, given what the witches had said. He even allows himself to ponder on the possibility of being king, but puts aside the thought of having to do anything dishonourable to achieve it, in the hope that it will 'just happen': 'If chance will have me king, why, chance may crown me, Without my stir.'

So, although some dramatic things have been said, nothing has upset the status quo. We know that Macbeth has allowed himself to entertain the idea of being king, but we know that he's just going to let things take their course. In terms of his *wants* or *needs* or *desires* we gather he desires to live up to his name (valiant, worthy, noble); but we've heard him consider (even though he's dismissed the thought) the possibility of dark deeds. So he's got ambition. The question that prompts it: which will win out, loyalty or ambition?

What the play is heading for is the moment when the balance is tipped: where Macbeth, by what he does (or, to be more precise, what he does *not* do), takes the first conscious step down the slippery path. This will be *the event that makes the play possible*. There are various terms for this. Film-makers call it the *Inciting Incident* (the moment that literally kick-starts the character into the action that will carry them through the play). I tend to use *The First Major Turning Point*. A nine-year old in a primary school, when I was talking about things that make stories work, called it *The Big Bit*, which I rather like.

So how does the Major Turning Point work? In Macbeth, for me, it is at the very end of Act 1, Scene 5. The king is coming to stay the night in Macbeth's castle. We've already overheard Lady Macbeth – having learned of what the witches had foretold – decide that her husband has got to seize the moment. The final exchange in the scene is a brilliant example of the kick-start moment.

> *Macbeth*: My dearest love.
>   Duncan comes here tonight.
> *Lady Macbeth*: And when goes hence?
> *Macbeth*: Tomorrow, as he purposes.
> *Lady Macbeth*: O, never
>   Shall sun that morrow see!

She then goes on to make it very clear that the only way Duncan is getting out of the castle is feet first. And what does Macbeth say? He says, 'We will speak further.' He doesn't say, 'I'm a good and loyal general, we'll have none of that talk.' He doesn't say, 'I've thought about that, but we'll just leave things to chance.' He says, 'We will speak further.' Then they leave. He's taken the first, conscious step, down the primrose path to hell. The status quo has shifted. Macbeth's twin (and conflicting) *drives* – wanting to be 'good' and wanting be 'great' – are at war within him. The latter has won out; he has made a conscious choice and the main action of the play is underway.

As a general principle, this First Major Turning Point can be characterised as:

- Having it's equivalent in all dramatic narratives.
- Happening somewhere not too far from the start of the play.
- Being something that the main characters are conscious of.
- Changing the status quo.

Example 71.2 *Little Red Riding Hood*

Macbeth is a grand, complex work. At the other end of the scale, the story of *Little Red Riding hood* is a relatively simple one, but one which teaches us as much about how story and character are inextricably linked. I have used Little Red frequently with groups of very young writers, but I also recommend it – and other folk/fairy tales – as a useful guide for anyone interested in developing a dramatic narrative.

Applying some of the things we've looked at earlier, let's see what we know about Little Red at the start of the story.

- She lives with her mother on the edge of a wood.
- Her grandmother lives by herself on the other side of the wood.
- Her grandmother is ill in bed.
- Her mother gives her a basket of food to take to her grandmother.
- Her mother makes her promise not to stray from the path, but to go straight through the wood.

That's all straightforward: small, obedient child given task to do by mother. And of course, the First Major Turning Point to the status quo is the moment when Little Red, tripping merrily through the forest with her basket of food, sees some flowers by the side of the path and wanders off into the woods to pick them. If Macbeth's action was to *not tell Lady Macbeth that there'll be no talk of murder under his roof*, Little Red's action is *to disobey her mother's wishes and please herself*. I think the interesting part of her action is the pleasing of herself. Generally the tale is held up as a little moral, telling young people that wolves will get them if they disobey the adults. It becomes a much more interesting story if it is seen as a rite-of-passage: that necessary time in the life of any young person when the inner instincts come into conflict with the world of adult authority. So, far from this being simply a naughty child soon to get her come-uppance, we begin to see someone whose drives are a conflict between what she *wants* (to be obedient) and what she *needs* (to follow her desires). We can go further and say that this is a conflict between her *conscious want* (to be obedient) and her *unconscious need* (to follow her desires). Wolves, granny-eating and axes are a result not just of the conscious flouting of parental authority; they flow from the unconscious assertion of the libido.

Outcome

We can now see that two very different stories, Macbeth and Little Red Riding Hood, are underpinned by similar guiding principles:

1 A status quo: loyal general supports king; single-parent family at home.

2 A day marked out as slightly different, with the possible outline of problems on the horizon: granny's ill at the other end of the forest; the witches tell the general he could be king himself.

3   A demonstration that the status quo will be upheld: the child promises to be obedient; the general puts wicked thoughts to the back of his head.

4   A conflict between the conscious and the unconscious drives, in which the unconscious makes itself known: 'I want to please myself, not mum'; 'I might very well kill the king in order to take his place.'

5   A conscious choice to do – or not to do – which brings about a change in the status quo: pick the flowers; not to rule out Lady Macbeth's suggestions.

6   Events which flow inevitably from step 5: granny gets eaten; Macbeth dies a murderer.

Exercise 72 Rewrite
Participants: All groups, individual

Go back to the character and the opening scene you developed. In the light of everything we have been thinking about, map out the play up to a possible First Major Turning Point. Do this in note form, and feel free to play around with a range of possibilities.

Exercise 73 Breaking the rules
Participants: All groups, individual

It may be that the style you are developing for your play is very different from the more classic model. Look at a range of contemporary plays and their opening sequences, scenes or chapters. See how the elements discussed in this chapter are at work. You will find that in a great deal of modern work (*Waiting for Godot*, by Samuel Beckett onwards) they are far less marked, often seemingly invisible, but it does not mean they are not there. If you have the opportunity to observe actors and a director at the start of the rehearsal, you will discover them asking many of the questions we have addressed in this chapter, even (or perhaps more particularly) those with more abstract narratives. If the writer has done the job well, the clues – however sparse – will be there for the actors to unearth.

Take a contemporary play that works in a non-naturalistic, abstract manner. Using the methods in this chapter, see how the writer has revealed aspects of the main character.

Example 73.1 *Attempts on her Life*, by Martin Crimp

The examples of narratives used so far have been very much in the classic mould and style. The play you wish to write may employ a more abstract style. *Attempts on her Life* seems to obey none of the dramatic principles we have been looking at. The 'her' of the title never appears, the world of the play seems utterly fractured, there seems to be no sense of turning points in the action.

The play opens with a collage of eleven separate messages on an answer-machine. They are all for a person called Anne. Through the course of the messages (mostly unnamed callers) a picture of Anne is built up; but it certainly doesn't give any sense of a 'well-rounded character'. It is almost as if each caller is speaking to a different person.

Call 1   Anne has been hurt by someone.
Call 2   Anne thinks someone is crazy.
Call 3   Anne has to pick up a truck and a 'device'.
Call 4   Anne has a mum.
Call 5   Anne can pick up the truck from the showroom.
Call 6   Anne is a 'fucking bitch'. Anne will soon be dead for things she did.
Call 7   Anne has sent a postcard and a (not immediately recognisable) photo of herself to her mum and dad. Anne has asked her mum and dad for money. Anne will not be receiving money from her mum and her dad.
Call 8   Anne is in the thoughts and prayers of some people.
Call 9   Anne has an invitation to call someone, and meet up.
Call 10 Anne is going to consent to sexual abuse.
Call 11 Anne is hiding from the world. Anne is crying for help. Anne used to make someone smile.

In terms of the status quo – the world of the play we are being introduced to – it seems that nothing is fixed. The first scene contains nothing of the easily identified, enclosed social worlds of *The Seagull* or *Death of a Salesman*; nor the clear myth-worlds of *Macbeth* or *Little Red Riding Hood*. It hasn't even the cohesion of the country lane we discover Estragon and Vladimir on. Instead it is the fractured one of modern electronic communications, timelines and multiple identities. If there is going to be a turning point that kick-starts the story, it might emerge from any of the fragments of information we are given in the first scene.

Outcome

On a first reading, it seems that the writer has thrown up an impenetrable smokescreen. But, as with the other examples, he has planted in 'facts' about the character: emotional life, social life, economic circumstances, etc. in the exposition. The status quo of the world *is* its fractured nature. In a world that is fragmented, *everything* is a turning point.

The play, in its very form and structure, mirrors the complexities of modern interactions (missed connections, multi-identities, shifting values). The writer, by seeming to break the rules/principles of more classic forms, is not denying them. He is commenting upon them. He clearly understood them. This will be useful to remember if your own play employs an unconventional style.

CONCLUSION

We have seen that by 'character' we mean much more than the person depicted. It is more to do with the way in which that person is revealed when put under pressure. The next step is to depict the journey that person is on, and what the outcome is.

It may be that you have already discovered the ending to the scene you have been writing (or even the play you want to write), even if you've no idea how to get there. Intuitive leaps of this kind often occur in the making of art – the moment when you instinctively know that humble-but-happy character X will end up as rich-but-miserable. Absolutely go with that instinct. It's what is called the 'Eureka moment' and it is an interesting illustration of the way in which the processes of imagination, learning and discovery in art and science are very similar.

So what is this 'Eureka moment'? The story goes that the Greek physicist Archimedes had been pondering on certain questions regarding volume and weight. A local king wanted to know how much pure gold was in his crown, but there seemed to be no way of ascertaining the volume of gold without melting down the crown. Getting into his bath one day, Archimedes noticed the water, as usual, rising as he lowered himself into it. What leapt into his mind on this occasion was the fact that the volume of water displaced was equal to the volume of the amount of the body part that was in the water. By measuring the amount of water displaced he could then have the volume of the body part. Ditto the crown. As this flash of insight occurred to Archimedes, he is said to yelled have 'Eureka!'

There are many examples of scientists claiming to have made that intuitive leap to the solution of a problem; just as there are of writers having 'got the ending' even though the whole story had not been written. In both cases, the task has been to go back and work the whole thing through again, to see if the final outcome – be it a dramatic conclusion or a scientific discovery – holds water, if you'll forgive the pun. So if the Eureka moment happens, go with it, always knowing that the hard work of 'proving' the case now has to take place.

Which leads us on to the next chapter.

5 Finding the story

As we have begun to discover, a story is an artificially constructed sequence of events that are rooted in the actions of the main character(s), or *protagonist(s)*, a term we will be using from now on. The word is from the Greek *protagonistes*, which is made up of *protos*, meaning 'first' and *agonistes*, meaning 'combatant'. So our protagonist is our 'first combatant', the one whose journey leads the action.

Actors do sometimes use the vocabulary of combat in relation to an audience, as in 'I knocked them dead in act five', or 'this play will really sock it to them'. The British actor Alec Guinness once remarked, 'Tackling a live audience is like fighting a wild animal'. I've always thought it rather curious that the audience is often characterised as the enemy, some sort of beast to be subdued and controlled. Although, as any actor will tell you, each audience does have its own sort of collective identity and that can range from rapt attention through to indifference and downright hostility. However, the notion of having our 'first combatant' is a useful one for our purposes. It reminds us that – as with an actual physical battle – a story is about planned, forward-moving activity that (a) is led by someone, (b) has a purpose, (c) involves some form of struggle, and (d) has an outcome.

In Chapter 1 we began to look at ways of finding story-shapes (for example, Exercise 27), and in Chapter 4 we looked in detail at the way in which a fully explored character can contain the seeds of a story. In this chapter, we will see how we can map out a complete narrative structure, and what basic principles operate under any story. This is the craft of attending to 'the solid carpentry of *imparting information* and *laying fuses*'.

It is interesting that the word 'carpentry' was used, but I think that it is very appropriate in that play*wrighting* – as opposed to the more internationally used play*writing* – is a craft. 'Wright' derives from Old English, Old Saxon and High German words indicating 'work' and 'making', and its dictionary definition is: 'a person who creates, builds, or repairs something specified: a playwright, shipwright' (Collins English Dictionary). Just as the maker of ships or chairs or knitted-jumpers must know the basic principles of the craft, so must the playwright understand those of their craft. This chapter will attend to the specifics of those principles.

CHANGE

Change happens all the time in a story. We have already dipped into the Major Turning Point and how that crucially affects the turn of events for the journey of the protagonist. As we shall see, every moment of a play is about change, and it happens on any number of levels.

Change operates at all levels of human experience: the inner changes of emotions, intellect, psychology and spirit, as well as the external and material changes. We can categorise these as:

External change:

- Change of status.
- Change of fortune.
- Change of circumstance.
- Change of allegiance.
- Change of role.
- Etc.

Internal change:

- Change of mood.
- Change of heart.
- Change of mind.
- Change of belief.
- Change of view.
- Change of affection.
- Etc.

The finding and the development of the narrative is welded to the changes happening with the protagonist(s); so from now on, in all the work we do, everything we have learned about character and the protagonist will be brought into the process.

Here are a couple of exercises exploring change happening within a single sequence, or scene.

Exercise 74 The empty room

Participants: All groups, individual (10–30 minutes)

As before, just follow the instructions and write down your immediate responses. The spontaneous response can often be the most creative one. Remember all the instant-writing/instant-character work already done.

1   Imagine an empty room. It can be anywhere in the world. There is nothing in it at all. There is a source of light (natural or artificial) and there is a way into the room. What is the shape of the room? What is it made from? What is the 'feel' of the room (smell, atmosphere, etc.)?

2   Now place an object in the room, something that could have been easily carried into it by one person. This object is going to be central to what happens next.

3   Now place a person in the room: Character X. Describe them in a little detail.

4   Now place a second person just outside the room and describe them in a little detail: Character Y.

5   Character Y enters the room.

6   Character X says something.

7   Character Y says something.

8   One of the characters leaves the room, with or without the object.

9   What type of change has happened?

As before, just follow the instructions and write down your immediate responses. The spontaneous response can often be the most creative one. Remember all the instant-writing/instant-character work already done.

Example 74.1

•   A tall narrow room. It is made of dark wood. Warm and dusty. A narrow window, high up on the wall. Very little light. A trap door.

•   A blonde, curly wig lies on the floor.

•   A large, pale-faced man sits in a corner. He wears a long, green robe. He is crying.

•   He is about 45. He picks up the wig and mops his eyes with it.

•   Outside the room is a bald woman. She is Scottish. She is in her 70s. She is wearing a dressing gown and slippers. She's got a lot of makeup on.

- The woman opens the trap door and comes into the room.
- WOMAN: Freddie, just give it back to me, your father will be arriving in half an hour.
- MAN: Mother, he's got every right to know, you should tell him and if you won't, then I will.
- The man picks up the wig and leaves the room.

Outcome

- Even though this has been 'instant writing' and we don't know anything more about the story, there has clearly been a change in the relations between the two people. The mother has made a demand, but the son has defied her and so her status has been lowered.
- We don't know anything more about the people in the sequence you have made, and we will leave them there. What you created was a short scene in which, through a simple exchange of dialogue, triggered by an object, there has been some sort of change taking place.

Exercise 75 More empty rooms
Participants: All groups, individual

1   Look at the list of all the ways a person can change *internally*, in the emotional, intellectual, psychological, moral or indeed spiritual sense. Change of mood, of mind, of view, of principle, of belief, etc.

2   Look at the list of all the ways *external* change can happen to someone. Change of status, of circumstance, etc.

3   Go back to the previous exercise. Create another room, an object, two people and the two lines of dialogue. Once again, don't plan too much at the start, just arrive at your room and your object quite spontaneously. When you get to the two people, allow yourself a little time to think about what *levels of change* are happening with both characters.

4   Try the 'empty room' exercise a few more times. Each time explore different levels of change that are happening with the characters. Stick to the same structure, but allow a little more dialogue in if that feels appropriate or useful. But remember that actions can speak louder than words.

Outcome

As I have said, and as we will see, in a fully developed play there is change happening all the time, from the small to the immense, from moment to moment, scene to scene and act to act. The playwright David

Hare once said: 'Never allow a character to leave a scene the same as they entered it.' There is always some shift, even if it is a slight one, which will take the story onwards. If a scene doesn't do that it is quite likely to be redundant, and even if we don't realise it as we are writing the play, you can be sure that good actors will sniff it out in rehearsals. I remember occasions when an actor has said, 'We don't learn anything new in the scene, so why is it here?' and we then cut it. I hadn't done my job properly and the actor's instinct was spot-on.

Exercise 76 Change beneath the surface

Participants: All groups, individual

Here is an exercise that allows you to explore psychological and emotional change through a surface 'activity'.

1 Write a list of ordinary, daily activities that can be shared. For example: making a bed, preparing a meal, laying a table, bathing the baby, clearing a classroom, getting the bar ready for opening time, stacking the shelves, playing cards, planning a route, etc.

2 Choose one. If it is a task you are familiar with, so much the better, as you will be familiar with the detail.

3 You are going to write a scene in which characters X and Y are both engaged in this activity.

4 Character X is 'in charge' and knows exactly what needs to be done. Character Y is the 'helper' and is not familiar with the process.

5 The dialogue is driven by the mechanics of the task in hand: questions, answers, mistakes, corrections, etc.

6 Once you have decided on the task and the two characters, start writing. Don't think about personality, psychology, etc. Don't over plan, just allow the scene to write itself out.

7 Don't try and force anything onto the scene, but if topics arise naturally out of the activity, then allow them in (for example, if the task is 'making the bed' and the sheets for the bed are old linen and belonged to great-grandma, then some discussion of her might be appropriate). But always keep the focus of attention on the task in hand. Write the scene through until the task is fully completed. Be as detailed as you can. (See Example 76.1.)

8 Look through the scene (or have it read out if you are working with a group). See what clues are in the scene as to what the relationship between the characters might be. (See Example 76.2.)

9   You are now going to think about a second draft of the scene. As before, the task will be completed from start to finish, so you know how the mechanics of the scene works. The focus of the scene will be on the task. This time though, there will be a *change in the relationship* between X and Y. Give the characters in the scene very strong objectives. Make notes on how the scene will develop. (See Example 76.3.)

Write the scene.

Example 76.1

Y: Carrot soup? Yum.
X: Just for you and me.
Y: Just us. I thought . . .
X: You cut the oranges, I'll peel the carrots.
Y: Oranges?
X: Oranges.
Y: In carrot soup?
X: Sure.
Y: Ugh.
X: Lovely.
Y: Ugh.
X: You wait. Pass me the knife.
Y: I thought you wanted me to cut the oranges.
X: That's the carrot knife. This is the orange knife.
Y: Does it matter?
X: In my kitchen it does.
Y: Little drink?
X: Too early.
Y: Let's open this little bottle . . .
X: No, no it's for the soup.
Y: Cognac in soup?
      Etc.

Example 76.2

Attitudes, characteristics and status issues have already begun to appear: Y is a bit conventional when it comes to soup making; it is X's kitchen and recipe and s/he is a bit territorial. In your own scene, allow such details to emerge. You will now have a scene in which an activity has been completed. You will also – thanks to the work done in the previous chapters – have some idea of who the characters are, what their relationship is, etc.

Example 76.3

- X wants to win the affections of Y through his/her sophisticated cookery skills.
- Y is not impressed and clearly regards X as a food-snob.
- The soup is foul and X is distraught.
- Y feels sorry for X, produces a can of tomato soup, heats it up and they talk about comfort food.
- X has shifted from attempting to control the situation to accepting help.
- Y has shifted from critical to compassionate.

Outcome

You will now have developed a scene in which there has been a significant change for the protagonists, signalled through the way a shared activity is negotiated. What you have been experimenting with is *subtext*, which is the next item on the menu.

SUBTEXT

Subtext: any meaning or set of meanings which is implied rather than stated in literary work, especially in a play. Read any play by Harold Pinter and you will find that the seemingly banal and 'surface' dialogue is actually loaded with implied meaning.

As any actor will tell you, the most interesting texts for them are those in which the true meanings of the lines they are delivering are 'under the surface' as it were. This is worth remembering, as it is actors for whom we are writing. Of course, there are the scenes and speeches where great inner truths are revealed, but as a general principle the actor will seek the 'what is not said', the stuff that is going on under the surface. In the plays by Harold Pinter you will see that the evasiveness of the dialogue and the carefully planted pauses are where the riches lie. Hamlet, even if he is actually spelling out all his thoughts, as characters in Shakespeare tend to, goes on at some length about the question of being or not being, but he fails to answer it. What is not said, not concluded, left open, is more interesting for the actor, and for the audience.

Here are some exercises that continue to explore the place of *change* in a scene, but with an emphasis on *subtext*. There will be a shared activity, but it will not be quite so obviously the motor of the scene as wigs and soup-making were in previous examples.

Exercise 77 Reading a newspaper
Part one

Participants: All groups

For this exercise you will need a range of newspapers of the day: broad-sheet and tabloid, local and national. Before starting, think a little about all the different things a newspaper contains: news items (wars, crime, celebrity goings-on, royal scandals, politics etc.), advertisements, letters, agony columns, editorials, crosswords, sport, etc. All or any of these will become the focus of the exercise.

1 Divide up into groups of three. Decide who is A, B and C. Each group has one newspaper (comic-book or magazine, etc., if appropriate to the group).

2 A and B will be 'readers'.

3 C will be an 'invisible recorder'. In this role, C will have a notepad and pen.

4 A and B will look through the newspaper and will have a conversation about items in it.

5 C will not participate in the conversation at all, but will remain as if invisible. The task is to jot down, in note form, the general development of the conversation. The emphasis is on 'note form'. There should be no anxiety about getting every single word down; the function of the notes is to record the main outline of what is said.

6 A and B should not feel they have to read the whole paper. The object is to allow the items they read to prompt their own thoughts, com-ments, memories and feelings. However, remember the exercise is called 'reading a newspaper'. The conversation will drift away from what is in the newspaper, but it should always return to that focus of attention.

7 The conversation should be allowed to go on for a good 10–15 minutes.

Example 77.1

This is and example of a type of full conversation that C would make notes on.

A: A hundred and ninety-seven million! That's gross!

B: [READS] 'Andrew Jack Whittaker was already blessed and he was wealthy by most standards when he turned up yesterday dressed in his trademark black, from the tip of his cowboy boots to his stetson hat . . . ' America, he's American, that explains it, that . . .

A: I bet there's people in England who'd do that, I bet . . .

B: Would you?

A: Dunno . . . no . . . it's gross. Look here, it says all those asylum seekers are destitute, it's not right, why should . . .

B: My dad says the asylum seekers . . .

A: So does mine, but that doesn't mean it's right. I told him his dad came to this country, so what does that make his dad?

B: Does your dad do the lottery?

A: He won ten pounds last week. Said he's used it for my birthday present.

B: Is it your birthday?

A: Saturday.

B: Let's look at the stars. What's your sign?

A: Capricorn.

B: I'm Virgo. I wish I were something else.

A: Hope he spends more than a tenner on me, I told him I wanted that latest . . .

B: Look at that dress Britney Spears has got on, I wish . . .

A: Britney Spears is rubbish.

B: I wonder what star sign she is?

A: I wouldn't be seen dead in a dress like that.

B: You couldn't afford a dress like that. My dad said . . .

A: She's jail bait.

B: My dad . . .

A: Here's the stars.
   Etc.

Part two

Participants: All groups

1 Each group will now have its conversation in note form.

2 The task now is for C to go through the notes, with A and B putting them in their own notebooks.

3 Now A, B and C will have an identical set of notes.

Part three

Participants: All groups

1 Everyone will now work singly, from the notes they have.

2 The notes will form the raw material for a conversation between two characters, A and B.

3 This time the characters are fictional.

4 Give the characters names and think of them as totally different from the people who had the original conversation. Use Exercises 22 and 23 in Chapter 1 to name the characters.

5 Look through the notes. See what sorts of things come up in the conversation. Are there topics that the two people keep coming back to? What is the general drift of the conversation?

6 See if the conversation and the things that are discussed give a clue as to what is going on *that is not talked about*. What might be going on under the surface? See if there are clues as to some sort of *change* that is happening to one or both of the characters.

7 Rewrite the conversation in the light of what you discovered in step 8.

8 If you find that the conversation is going off into new and interesting territory, allow it to do so. Remember that you always have the notes to support you if you feel stuck.

9 Work hard to keep the things that are *really* being expressed under the surface, in the subtext. Think of 'hint', 'almost say', 'suggest', as opposed to 'tell', 'confess', 'explain'.

10 Remember that the task is not to reproduce the original conversation, but to use it as an inspiration to develop a new one.

11 Find a way for the scene to conclude.

Example 77.2

- Look for something in the scene that is half-referred to (asylum seekers) or is conspicuous by its absence (no mention of mums).

- Use that as a clue to what you decide is going on under the surface. Let's take mums. Why are they never mentioned? What is the story there?

- Insert into the background story the fact that character B's mum has recently died.

- Rewrite the scene bearing in mind that both characters are very aware of this fact, but are avoiding it. We've all been in social situations where a subject we want to steer clear of keeps making itself known, despite all our efforts. This is one of those. Already character A's line 'I wouldn't be seen dead in a dress like that' becomes very loaded.

- Explore the tension between *not* talking about B's mum and B's possible (unconscious) *need* to talk about her mum.
- In terms of *change*, see if there is a moment when B's need to talk about her mum bursts through the surface: where she moves from denial to the beginnings of acceptance.

Outcome

You now have a scene in which a conversation prompted by a newspaper has allowed you to play with the notion of subtext. From this point on, in all the work, we will constantly hold onto the notion of *change* and *subtext*.

Exercise 78 Looking at a view
Part one
Participants: All groups

This exercise follows on from the last, in that it deals purely with subtext. There is no actual physical activity, no wigs, soup or newspapers, just two people looking at a view and having a conversation. It will be an opportunity to fully explore 'the stuff that is going on under the surface'.

1 Work in groups of three.

2 A and B will be the speakers, C the 'invisible note-taker'.

3 Find a view. If you are working in a building, find a window to look out of onto a view that has a variety of things of interest (a busy street, a playground, a park). If you can go outside, go into the park itself, or any public place. Whatever you choose, try for a view that is (a) public, (b) exterior and (c) includes the sky.

4 As with the previous exercise, A and B talk to each other, and C invisibly records in note form.

5 Again, the object is to simply allow the view to stimulate the conversation, but allowing what is seen to stimulate other thoughts, memories, etc. Again, always come back to 'the view' as the focus of attention.

Example 78.1

This is an example of a type of full conversation that C would make notes on.

Two people are standing on a riverbank with a view of trees.

A: What sort of tree is that?

B: An elm?

A: Elm. That's a strange word.

B: Is it an elm?

A: It's not oak.

B: It's not an elm.

A: It's not a yew.

B: Yew?

A: They're found in graveyards.

B: That's a playing field, it's not a graveyard.

A: Could've been, once. There's a church over there.

B: Did you ever see that film? Where their house was on the site of a graveyard, the dead came back through the floorboards.

A: Scary.

B: Would you come here in the dark?

A: Not if I was drunk.

B: Why not?

A: Might fall in the river.

B: Doesn't look very deep.

A: No.

Long silence.

B: What's it called?

A: Dunno. It's more of a stream, really.

B: River, I'd say.

Silence.

A: Got any gum?

B: Yeah.

A: Look.

B: What?

A: On the bridge. Someone fishing. I wouldn't want to eat a fish out of there.

B: Why not?

A: There's those factories the other way. There'd be all the muck coming out of them.

Etc.

Part two

Participants: All groups

1 Each group will now have its own set of notes.

2 The task now is for A and B to copy down the notes made by C.

3 A, B and C now have identical sets of notes.

Part three

Participants: All groups

1 Everyone now works on their own.

2 The characters are now fictional. Name them.

3 You will invest one of the characters with a pre-occupation: something that is weighing on their mind and will affect their mood, their language, etc. This will not be directly communicated in the dialogue, but which will inform what they say and how they say it. (See Examples 78.1.)

4 You are going to write a scene in which 'nothing happens'. Again, the original conversation is there to support you, not to be reproduced. Keep it as ordinary as possible, by imagining it as an early scene in a play: any big revelations will happen later on in the play.

5 See what imagery is there that can be used and adapted to serve the needs of rewrite. (See Example 78.2.)

6 See if, in the course of the conversation, there is a change that takes place within the characters, and how this might affect the things that are said. Explore the subtext but avoid any melodramatic effects. (See Examples 78.3.)

7 Finish the scene with one of the characters leaving.

Examples 78.1

- The character has recently been told she has a life-threatening illness.
- The character has just won a fortune on the lottery.
- The character has just failed her exams.
- The character's pet dog has just died.
- The character has recently fallen in love.
- The character is falling in love with the other character.
- Etc.

Example 78.2

- There has been a great deal about death in the conversation so far, so I would invest one of the characters with a negative pre-occupation; recent news of a life-threatening condition, for example.
- See how the imagery of the view informs the subtext. Yew trees and graveyards have begun that process from the start.

Examples 78.3

- Does the other character begin to suspect that there is something wrong?
- A possible change for the character with the 'unspoken pre-occupation' might be: the beginnings of an acceptance of death.

Outcome

You have now written a scene in which, seemingly, nothing happens. You are in good company. When Samuel Beckett's *Waiting for Godot* first performed in London, in 1955, one of the (many) hostile critics said, 'Nothing happens. Twice.' Come to think of it, the situation in the example – two unknown people looking at a view – is not dissimilar to the one Beckett presents us with. The scene he sets is simply: *A country road. A tree. Evening.* We meet two tramps waiting for someone. By the end of the play they are still there and they are still waiting. I suspect that why the play, when first seen, was attacked was because it was seen as 'breaking all the rules'. I have already quoted the advice to, 'never allow a character to leave a scene the same as when they entered it'. *Waiting for Godot* is a play in which two characters leave a whole play in exactly the same circumstances as when they entered it. But the point is, rules are there to be broken – but we can break them only if we know them inside-out. Beckett certainly knew 'the rules' (or the underlying principles of classic dramatic structure), being a classical scholar, and it was because of this that he was able to write the 'anti-classic' play. Which is a good moment to begin to discuss structure: the task – mentioned earlier – of 'the solid carpentry of imparting information and laying fuses'.

STRUCTURE 1: IMPARTING INFORMATION

Exposition: the opening part of a play or a story, in which we are introduced to the characters and their situation.

We have already looked at ways in which the protagonists are introduced to us at the start of a play. What the playwright is doing is 'exposing' those things about the characters and their situation that will help the audience engage with the story at this point. However, there may be other key 'facts' that are not directly about the characters, but which the writer needs to let the audience know. These relate to 'the world of the play'.

Exercise 79 Exposition – the world of the play

Participants: All groups, individual

1   Take a few plays – classic, modern classic, contemporary – and read their opening sequences.

2   Note those facts about the world of the play that the writer has dropped into the dialogue.

3   Note the different techniques the writers use.

Example 79.1 *Romeo and Juliet*

This is exposition at its baldest. A prologue of fourteen lines is spoken, in which the whole story is told and the whole world of the play revealed.

> Two households, both alike in dignity,
> In fair Verona, where we lay our scene,
> From ancient grudge, break to new mutiny,
> Where civil blood makes civil hands unclean.
> From forth the fatal loins of these two foes
> A pair of star-crossed lovers take their life'
> Whose misadventured piteous overthrows
> Do with their death bury their parent's strife.
> The fearful passage of their death-marked love,
> And the continuance of their parent' rage,
> Which, but their children's end, nought could remove,
> Is now the two hours' traffic of our stage;
> The which if you with patient ears attend,
> What here shall miss, our toil will strive to mend.

This style of exposition does away entirely with the need for the audience to discover *what* happens. It tells us what *will* happen, so focussing us totally on *how* it happens.

Example 79.2 *Macbeth*

In the first two scenes – before we meet our 'first combatant' – we learn a number of things about the world of the play:

·   It has supernatural dimensions, in the form of witches.

·   There has been a great and bloody battle between the Scottish king's forces and those of the rebels, who are supported by the Norwegians.

- The thane of Cawdor has been a major rebel.
- The forces of the king have won the day, largely thanks to Macbeth, and the Norwegian king must pay 'ten thousand dollars' to the victors before he can bury his dead.
- Cawdor is to be put to death.

Here we have a broad canvas, on which a world of feudal brutality and supernatural creatures is depicted. In these two scenes we are told about what *has just happened*. It seems that everything has been put to rights, the good have been rewarded and the bad have got their just resorts. But what about those witches . . . ?

Example 79.3 *The Seagull*

In the scene with Medvedenko and Masha we not only learn about them (from what they say about themselves and each other), but are also given the low-down on two of the major protagonists, Nina and Konstantin. Chekhov has set the scene in the grounds of an estate, and in the background is a makeshift stage. There are some workmen in the background, completing the stage. We learn the following:

- There's going to be a play happening very soon.
- Konstantin has written the play.
- Nina will act in the play.
- Nina and Konstantin are in love.

Here we are being told what *is going to happen next*. We are also invited into a world of some wealth and privilege, with a smattering of 'the arts' thrown in.

Example 79.4 *Death of a Salesman*

In a previous exercise we looked at everything we learned about Willy, from what he said about himself and what Linda said about him. This is a scene with an enormous amount of information in it, and from our knowledge of Willy alone, we are given a detailed picture of his world. As the dialogue moves along though, Arthur Miller fleshes out the picture of his domestic world: this is not just *this* travelling salesman, it is the travelling salesman who lives in *this* house in *this* neighbourhood:

- Building developments have boxed the house in, so that even with the windows open there is no air.
- The street is lined with cars, there's no fresh air in the neighbourhood. The grass in the yard doesn't grow anymore.

- The builders cut the trees down.
- There used to be lilac, wisteria, peonies and daffodils growing, but these days not even a carrot would grow in the yard.
- The smell from apartments invades the house.

Here we are being invited to imagine *what was* in comparison to *what is*. This is the physical arena in which Willy's story unfolds, as it was once and as it is now.

Example 79.5 *Attempts on her Life*

In a previous exercise we looked at how hard facts (or what *seem* to be hard facts) about Anne are delivered in the first scene. We also noted that the very structure of the scene – a sequence of seemingly unconnected telephone messages – gave us a picture of a fragmented world of electronic communication. In terms of the wider world of the story, what other clues has the writer planted into the messages:

- This world embraces a number of (possible) places: Vienna, Prague, Minnesota, airports.
- This is a world in which intimate words (crude or sincere) and thoughts are received through anonymous machines.
- This is a world where the identity of the protagonist is constantly shifting, depending on the individual speaking to her through the machine.

You could call this anti-exposition, the polar opposite to the prologue in *Romeo and Juliet*. We are presented with a world where nothing can be taken at face value. We think we 'know' something about the protagonist, through the words of one caller, then all seems contradicted when the next caller comes on line. In its language and its references, this is the contemporary world we inhabit. Of all the plays we have looked at, it should present the most familiar world to us. However, in its evasiveness, it feels the least familiar, which is why it is so brilliant. It takes the world we *think* we know and exposes it as something utterly unknowable. Even the strange, bloody and supernatural world of *Macbeth* seems more solid than the shifting sands of the modern, techno-fragmented world of *Attempts on her Life*.

Example 79.6 *Little Red* and other tales

Look at any folk or fairy tale and you will find the same elements featured in the exposition: (a) specific protagonists with distinct character-features and (b) a specific world for the character to move in.

There was once upon a time a little country girl, born in a village, the prettiest little creature that ever was seen. Her mother was beyond reason excessively fond of her, and her grandmother yet much more. This good woman caused to be made for her a little red riding-hood; which made her look so very pretty, that everybody called her, the Little Red Riding hood. One day, her mother said to her . . .

(Iona and Peter Opie. *The Classic Fairy Tales*)

Once there was an old boatman who lived in a little hut on the banks of the holy River Ganges. For many, many years his family had rowed boats across the great river. His grandfather and his father had been boatmen before him; and our friend had taken over the job when he was just a boy. Like all the villagers he was poor. The money he made rowing people from one bank to the other could scarcely feed his family. But although life was hard he never grumbled. He was happy to be of service to his passengers. One day, a well-dressed city gentleman climbed into his boat . . .

(Beulah Candeppa. *Tales of South Asia*)

Once upon a time there lived an old man and his wife. The old man was of a kindly nature and had a pet sparrow which, since he was childless, he treated as tenderly as if it had been his own child. One day the old man took a basket and a hatchet in his hand and went as usual to the mountains to cut firewood. The old woman in the meantime began to wash clothes at the well . . .

(Iwaya Sazanami. *Japanese Fairy Tales*)

There was a man long ago living near Ballaghadereen named Owen O'Mulready, who was a workman for the gentleman of the place, and was a prosperous, quiet, contented man. There was no one but himself and his wife Margaret, and they had a nice little house and enough potatoes in the year, in addition to their share of wages, from their master. There wasn't a want or anxiety on Owen, except one desire, and that was to have a dream – for he had never had one. One day, when he was digging potatoes . . .

(Joseph Jacobs. *Celtic Fairy Tales*)

Outcome

With the examples I have used, and others you may have chosen, we have seen that the function of the exposition is to *prepare the ground*, by introducing the protagonist(s) and their world. Within this, some form of future dilemma, problem or question is raised (whether explicitly or just hinted at). Whatever the case, the writer has carefully chosen which facts from the back-story to expose. We have seen how this can be done by spilling all the beans at once (*Romeo and Juliet*) or by holding the cards very close to the chest (*Attempts on her Life*), and everything else in between. *Death of a Salesman* is a good example of how the modern 'well-made play' delivers its exposition – by enfolding the information very cleverly into the dialogue: we are receiving a huge amount of 'facts' without being aware of it.

Exercise 80 An opening passage

Participants: All groups, individual

You are going to write three opening passages for a play. In them you will be introducing your protagonist. Nothing hugely dramatic should happen, but you have to include a number of expositional 'facts' that the audience needs to know. The task is to insert them craftily, in such a way that the audience is not sitting there thinking, 'Oh we're being spoon-fed the facts.' Here are the 'facts' about the characters and the basic situation. Having done all the previous work on character, change and subtext, bring as much of that into the exercise as is useful. By now you should be adept at summoning up characters and situations quite speedily.

1   She went to college to study fine art. She likes the colour red. Her father died when she was eight years old. The college she studied at was a hotbed of left-wing politics. *Write this as her side of a telephone conversation.*

2   He was a singer in a college rock-band. He failed to complete the college course. He is overweight. He spoke at her mother's funeral. *Write this as two people who are talking about him (he is not present).*

3   She lived abroad for several years. While she was abroad there was civil unrest in her homeland. While she was abroad she met up with an old friend. She reads detective novels. She returned home as the successful executive for a large corporation. *Write this as a dialogue over dinner.*

Exercise 81 A prologue

Participants: All groups, individual

1   Find a news-story from the daily paper.
2   Imagine you are going to write a full play based on the story.

3   Write a prologue in which, as with *Romeo and Juliet*, you give the bare bones of the whole story, laying out *what* will happen to the characters, but not *how* it will happen.

Exercise 82 Character from Chapter 4
Participants: All groups, individual

Go back to the character and story-idea you were working on in Chapter 4. You wrote an opening scene, and it contained at least two characters. Consider everything we have done so far regarding opening scenes and their function. Rewrite the scene, bearing in mind the following:

1   What do we learn about the characters in terms of (a) what they say about themselves and (b) what the other characters say about them?

2   What change(s) takes place for the characters in terms of their situation?

3   How is the world of the play revealed?

4   How is subtext dealt with; how much is revealed by what is not said, half-said, alluded to and hinted at?

5   What questions does the scene summon up (consciously or otherwise) in the minds of the audience?

Exercise 83 Unpacking the suitcase
Participants: All groups, individual

We have discussed exposition as happening at the start of the play, but that is not the whole of it. In Chapter 4, we saw how the whole life history of the protagonist(s) needs to be in place before the story begins. It was as if you were packing a suitcase full of the character's whole existence and world and then, in scene one, deciding which items to take out and expose to the audience. But it does not finish there, for as you go along there will be other items in the suitcase that you will need to reveal to the audience at key moments in the play. So exposition continues – on different levels – throughout the play.

Look at a range of plays (or TV soap operas and dramas) and see how the writer has 'gone back to the suitcase' at certain points, to push the story forward and deepen our understanding of the protagonist(s). What devices and techniques have they used?

Examples 83.1

- In a melodrama (a type of sensational drama, with rather two-dimensional characters, popular in nineteenth-century Europe and America), the use of 'big, dramatic revelation' was common. The curtain on Act 1 might come down on a line such as, 'But Sir Roger, your long-lost father has been locked in the attic for these past fifty years!' Crude as this might seem, it tells us exactly what exposition is: those things that are brought in from the past lives of the protagonists to affect the on-stage action.

- When Macbeth seems to be faltering in his resolve to murder the king, Lady Macbeth reveals something about her own history to prove how much her own determination should spur him on:

> I have given suck, and know
> How tender 'tis to love the babe that milks me:
> I would, while it was smiling in my face,
> Have plucked my nipple from his boneless gums,
> And dashed the brains out, had I so sworn as you
> Have done to this.
>
> (Act 1, Scene 7)

- Exposition arrives in all sort of forms: the arrival of messages with hitherto unknown but crucial information (letters, faxes, phone messages, etc.); 'I remember' speeches; flashbacks; the use of a narrator-figure; confessions; gossip; the arrival of the messenger to tell the king that the enemy are outside the walls.

- Soap operas are practically all exposition. Note the way in which characters are continually sidling up to each other with the line, 'Sid, can I, er, have a word with you about what happened last night . . .' which is generally some bit of gossip about the shady goings on of one of the other characters.

Outcome

As you develop your play, bear in mind the use of ongoing exposition; how it continually dips into the suitcase to drive the action forward and deepen our knowledge of the protagonists. And by far the most important items in that suitcase, in terms of how the narrative will unfold from this point, are their deepest wants, needs and desires. What the protagonists *want* – their *drives* – is going to be the key to your structure from this point on.

STRUCTURE 2: FUSES AND BOMBS

The structure of the play and its forward drive are essentially bound up with the lives and actions of the protagonists. A small detail you have inserted into the exposition – a piece of information, a chance remark, a seemingly innocent action – can have huge repercussions later on in the play. What you are doing is laying fuses and planting unexploded bombs. Once again, every detail is there for a purpose.

In Chapter 4 we did some work around The First Major Turning Point: that moment in the play when the protagonist 'steps off the path' – literally in the case of Little Red Riding Hood, morally in the case of Macbeth. In both cases it was a result of a conflict of interests. The status quo is at risk. Little Red's wish to follow her mother's instructions loses out to her desire to pick the flowers. Macbeth's first step down the path to eternal damnation is when desire for earthly glory won out on his wish to be a good and loyal servant of his king.

The fact that I have just used the phrase 'in the case of' is perhaps not coincidental. One way of looking at a play is as a 'case study': an examination of how specific characters operate under specific circumstances. The psychoanalyst puts the spotlight on the patient's past in order to see how the influences of the past (and the choices of action/non-action in life flowing from that) have led to the present. The playwright creates fictional characters to do very much the same; that is, to see what led up to the *outcome*. How will it all turn out?

'The ending is everything' is something you will hear fiction writers saying. If the ending (conclusion, resolution, finale or payoff) is to be truly satisfying, it has to be absolutely rooted in its beginning. That is why we have spent so much time on life histories, exposition, status quo, etc. It's rather like building a house: great walls, beautiful roof, but if it's built on sand it'll just topple over. A play, like a building, is an act of architecture.

From now you will be working from the character, scene and story-idea you began to develop in Chapter 4. I'll be asking you to develop them in classic form – that is, where character development and narrative development are intertwined, in linear form. You may finally subvert that form, just as Samuel Beckett did. But if we do accept that we are working with a craft (remember '-wright' as opposed to '-write'?) then we can subvert only if we know the basic principles.

Exercise 84 The conflict between the conscious and the unconscious

Participants: All groups, individual

1   Go back to the characters you developed in the Chapter 4 exercises. Consider what their conscious wants (needs, desires, etc.) are at the start of the story. The character I briefly developed in that chapter – Taresh – might say, 'To be able to obtain those little things I need which would make my life bearable: bits of tobacco, enough money for the opera.'

2   Now think about what their unconscious wants might be. Taresh's might be to regain the self-respect he once felt.

3   Now think about what the conflict between the two might be. With Taresh, I would suggest that, if he were to go down the path of petty theft, the further he would take himself away from the possibility of self-respect.

Don't worry too much at this point if you are not sure what the unconscious desire or need is. Part of the task of writing a first draft is to discover your characters and your story. It might be that you won't discover key things until after you have finished the draft. But bear in mind the fact that all stories are – to greater or lesser degrees – based upon the conflict between what the protagonists *consciously think they want*, and what they *unconsciously desire*. A character might express himself as good and loyal, and might be perceived so in his actions by the other characters. Where the drama lies is in seeing if, when exposed to temptations, 'road blocks', new opportunities, etc., the sleeping inner desires are aroused. There is an interesting moment early in *Macbeth*, where the king is speaking of the traitor Cawdor, who had been previously one of the most trusted:

> There's no art
> To find the mind's construction in the face:
> He was a gentleman on whom I built
> An absolute trust.
>
> (Act 1, Scene 4)

Immediately Macbeth enters and the king says how much he values him and how much he owes him, to which Macbeth replies:

> The service and the loyalty I owe,
> In doing it, pays itself. Your highness' part
> Is to receive our duties; and our duties
> Are to your throne and state, children and servants . . .

Here we have Macbeth expressing his conscious values and intentions, juxtaposed with the example of a Cawdor: a man equally trusted by the king, but who harboured in his 'mind's construction' other values entirely. And we know what is going to happen when we get to the Major Turning Point, where Macbeth fails to make it very clear to Lady Macbeth that there will be no talk of murder. With Macbeth, the conflict between the conscious and the unconscious is huge. This is because as the unconscious desire (power, earthly glory) makes itself known and asserts itself through his actions, the protagonist's self-awareness that he is heading for eternal damnation grows and grows. At all points along the way he struggles with this: in Act 1, Scene 7 he says to Lady Macbeth, 'We will proceed no further in this business', only to be provoked further down the road when she makes the speech about dashing her baby's brains out.

So the conflict between the conscious and the unconscious is essentially one of *values*. Without this struggle there would be no drama. With Macbeth it is the fight between those values he knows are right, both socially (feudal loyalty) and morally (Christian duty), and the stakes are very high. In a different type of story, we might have a high-living, self-indulgent person whose unconscious need is to live a simple, spiritual life. Once again, the drama would lie in that person's resistance to that need, and how it wins out – or fails to.

Exercise 85 Continuing the conflict
Participants: All groups, individual

What we are discovering is that the 'character' of the protagonist is revealed by their *choice of action* – what they consciously do, or fail to do. And these actions are revealed when they are put under some sort of pressure. The pressure can be Little Red's desire to please herself and pick the pretty flowers, so leaving the straight path her mother has instructed her to stay on; or Lady Macbeth's taunt that her husband is less up to the task than she is.

So, the structure of a play can be seen as a progression of conflicts, in which the protagonist deals with the increasing pressures between the conscious and the unconscious. You could call this the *arc of the story*: the progression of events that take the protagonist from status quo to final outcome.

Without going into a developed story at all, draw up a list of conscious (C) and unconscious (U) drives or goals a protagonist might have. Make them as opposite as possible, so that the fuses for conflict are laid.

Examples 85.1

* (C) I refuse to work, (U) I want to be respected.
* (C) I must be a loyal wife, (U) I desire my freedom.
* (C) I need a quiet life, (U) I want adventure.
* (C) I want power, (U) I need to be loved.
* (C) I want adventure, (U) I need a quiet life.
* (C) I must be a good father, (U) I want to be a child again.
* (C) I am a forgiving human being, (U) I need revenge.
* Etc.

Exercise 86 Developing the battle

Participants: All groups, individual

Take a couple of the examples from the above list. Jot down the possible answers to the following questions. Allow them to help you to imagine a journey the protagonist is on.

1   How will the unconscious goal be revealed?

2   Will the protagonist embrace and accept the unconscious goal?

3   What steps will the protagonist take to avoid the unconscious goal?

4   What obstacles are placed along the way to prevent the protagonist achieving the unconscious goal?

5   Does the protagonist achieve/fail to achieve the unconscious goal?

6   What does it cost the protagonist to achieve/fail to achieve the unconscious goal?

7   What has been the big change in the character of the protagonist between the outset and the status quo and the resolution of the final outcome?

Example 86.1

Take my example of the '"I must be a loyal wife" (C), "I desire my freedom" (U)'. When thinking about the character, remember all the work done earlier on *specificity*: this is not just any wife, but this particular one.

- A single friend of hers has won a free holiday for two, to Greece.
- She says she can't take time off, as the small business she and her husband own is not doing so well.
- She finds at the back of her cupboard the old back-pack she used when she was a student.
- She takes the back-pack to the Oxfam shop.
- In the Oxfam shop she finds a pile of old records, dating back to her hippie days. She buys them.
- She plays the record for her husband, who says the business is doing really badly and scoffs at her for wasting money on old junk.
- They discuss the business and how to get through the year.
- The friend rings from the airport.
- Etc.

The final outcome would demonstrate how she does, or does not, achieve freedom. What you are plotting are those moments of change (or refusal to change) which take her towards, or away from, her desire for freedom.

Outcome

The answering of all these questions will provide you with the basis for the architecture of your story. It should be clear by now that the journey of the protagonist, character, story and plot are totally bound up with each other. In Chapter 1, we noted that 'to plot' a play is just that: the playwright is conspiring to completely involve the unsuspecting audience in her fiction. She draws them in with the characters she reveals, she hooks them with the conflicts in the story, she traps them in the unfolding plot. She rewards them with a satisfying outcome.

THE FINAL OUTCOME

The phrase 'the ending is all', has been mentioned. We all know when we feel cheated by an ending. That doesn't mean that the 'good' character has to necessarily come off well, or that a 'bad' one has to get his just desserts. It's more to do with instinctively knowing that the ending is just not 'true' to the drama that has been unfolding, when we know we have somehow been cheated by the payoff. There was a time when 'happy endings' were written into some of Shakespeare's tragedies, and Cordelia doesn't die and it all ends merrily after the mayhem. There were Hollywood films (in the 1940s and 1950s particularly) in which the censors, as guardians of a state-imposed morality, would not allow the villain to get away with the crime, even when everything about the story said things were heading that way.

It is something to do with the ending having to feel *appropriate* to everything that has led up to it. If the three sisters, in Chekhov's play, had packed their bags and got on the train to Moscow at the end, we might not feel so sad for them, but we'd feel totally let down by the playwright.

So what makes an ending 'appropriate'? Why is it appropriate that the girl should get the boy in *As You Like It*, that the lovers should die in *Romeo and Juliet*, that the murderer gets caught in any Agatha Christie play, and that Oedipus should gouge his eyes out? We, the audience *don't know* if Rosalind will get Orlando, but everything prompts us to believe she will and we want to know *how*. We *do* know that Romeo and Juliet end up dead (the Prologue has told us), but again we want to know *how*. We don't know *who* did the murder on the Orient Express, but we want to know *who* and *why*. We don't know *why* a terrible fate awaits Oedipus, but we want to know *what* it will be. We know that Little Red has placed herself and her grandmother in terrible danger, and we want to know *if* and *how* she gets them all out of it.

The appropriate ending is the ending that (a) answers the questions that are summoned up in our minds by the beginning, but (b) is arrived at in ways we did not expect.

Example 86.2

Let's take the earlier example of the woman who consciously wants to be a loyal wife, but who unconsciously desires her freedom. Taking on board all that we've done around character-creation, world of the story etc., let's imagine we've got her to the First Major Turning Point: the moment where she goes off the path from loyal wifehood and recognises that there are other things she wants from life. The questions that are summoned up are (a) will she get what she wants? (b) how will she get what she wants? and (c) what does she *really* want? This last is very important, because it might be that what she *really* wants is to be a loyal wife *and* have her freedom. So the endings for this story – all appropriate to the dilemma that her conscious/unconscious load on her at the start – could be any of the following:

- After a series of setbacks and struggles she discovers a new life on a Greek island with another free spirit.

- After a series of setbacks and struggles she settles for a new life on a Greek island that is a replica of her old life in the London suburbs.

- After a series of setbacks and struggles she resigns herself to her old life back in the London suburbs.

- After a series of setbacks and struggles she realises her true freedom lies with her old life back in the London suburbs.

- Etc.

Outcome

Any of these endings would have (a) answered the questions that were summoned up for us at the start and – if they had kept us guessing – (b) given us the answers *in ways we do not expect*. This is an interesting one, and a challenging one for a writer. I personally love the idea of someone who is trapped by the notion of 'loyalty' (duty, responsibility, etc.) going off and eventually finding individual freedom on a Greek island; but as a dramatic conflict it feels rather thin. On the other hand, the notion of someone who wants all that, but who returns to 'what is known' and accepts it as a sort of 'freedom' is not something that appeals personally; but it contains more interest on a dramatic level.

A play by Noel Coward, which eventually became a film called *Brief Encounter*, comes to mind. It is the story of a suburban English housewife in the 1940s. She meets a stranger (a doctor, also married) in the buffet of a train station. Over a series of encounters they fall in love. Everything in us wants them to kick over the traces and make a new life together. Everything in the story is telling us that it is impossible – the society they live in, the innate self-repression of the protagonists, the moral codes of the time – and we know that it is doomed. We know that it will end terribly. What we want to know (against every hope) is *how*. The brilliance of the story is that we instinctively *know* how it will end, and the hook is we don't know *how*. At all points in the narrative, the protagonists could say, 'What the hell, let's just run off together,' but given their natures and the world they inhabit, we would be very let down if they had done so – much as we would like them to.

The old phrases 'keeping the audience on the edge of their seats' (thriller) and 'they were rolling in the aisles' (comedy) tell us a lot. One is about the suspense of the expectation (who did it, etc.); the other is about the surprise of the unexpected. In both cases the audience is being 'set up', and finally gets what they want – a gasp of surprise or a good laugh – *but in ways they did not expect.*

Exercise 87 Moments of change

Participants: All groups, individual

Go back to your own protagonist and the story you have been developing since Chapter 4.

1   Think again about what the conscious/unconscious drives or goals of the protagonist are.

2   Take a pile of postcards/index cards.

3   Write down what might be 'moments of change' for the protagonist. Remember that by 'change' we can mean change on any level – emotional, social etc. – but that it happens through some sort of pressure placed upon the character, and a choice they make.

4   Lay the cards out in a line, in the sequence they occur in the story. Mark the ones that indicate major moments of change, where the protagonist is under most pressure (MPM).

5   As a general principle, the 'major-pressure' moments (MPM) will be spaced out fairly evenly along the line. If they all occur at the start, or are all bunched together in the middle, then perhaps something is wrong with the structural rhythm of the piece. The drama lies in the mounting difficulties the protagonist encounters, and how they are dealt with. Try moving the cards around, to see if MPM(d) should come before MPM(b), etc.

6   Make it difficult for *all* the characters. Apply the same tests to their journeys.

Outcome

If you have already achieved the 'Eureka' moment, in which the final outcome has revealed itself, this is the point where you have the opportunity to test it out. If your character really *is* a mass murderer who ends up making a speech from the scaffold, then the cards will tell you if you are on the right track or not. It may be, as the story stands, that the mass-murderer scenario is entirely ludicrous. However, it may be that you absolutely want that to be the outcome, in which case now is the time to re-construct everything leading up to it. You are the goddess of the world you are making. As long as that world is true to its own rules, you can re-shape it to your will.

Exercise 88 Story model
Part one
Participants: All groups, individual

We have already explored various ways to create a whole story. Here is another model exercise, through which you can apply the work done in this chapter and theprevious one.

The first steps in the exercise are to answer questions. Stick to the externals as far as possible, describing from the outside. Be quite brief, but be specific. Don't go into the character's inner lives or psychology. Adopt a journalistic approach. (See Examples 88.1 and 88.2.)

1   Think of a household and its members. Have three or four people living there. Keep it quite ordinary. Answer the following questions about the household.
    •   Where is it located and what type of dwelling is it?
    •   What sort of condition is it in?
    •   Who are its members?

2   There is no food in the household.
    •   What sort of food is usually found there?
    •   Why is there no food today?

3   Someone leaves to go in search of food.
    •   Who is s/he?
    •   Why does this particular person go?
    •   What sort of food is s/he looking for?
    •   Where is s/he heading?

4   After some difficulty s/he manages to obtain some food.
    •   How does s/he obtain the food, and by what means?
    •   Where does s/he obtain the food?
    •   What sort of food does s/he obtain?

5   On the way back s/he is delayed.
    •   How is s/he delayed?
    •   By whom or what is s/he delayed?
    •   Where is s/he delayed?

6 When s/he finally gets back, the place is deserted.

- Why is it deserted?
- Where have the other members of the household gone?

7 Is the outcome of the story a change for the better, or a change for the worse, in the lives of the characters? (See Examples 88.3.)

Example 88.1

- It is a flat at the top of a tower block, on an estate in south London.
- It is very tidy, but there is damp on some of the walls.
- It is a family of asylum seekers: two parents, two children and a grandmother.

Example 88.2

- They generally eat cheap canned food.
- Today they have run out of coupons.

Examples 88.3

- If the outcome were a change for the better, the other members of the family may have left a note saying that their application for asylum had been granted, they had gone to look at better accommodation, and the father was now free to obtain employment.
- If the outcome were a change for the worse (unfortunately more likely), the authorities would have arrived to inform the family that they were to be deported, and to remove them from the premises.

Outcome

You now have the skeleton of a story, based upon (a) a given situation, (b) a problem, (c) a sequence of actions, and (d) a final outcome.

Part two – story model and character
Participants: All groups, individual

You are now going to add flesh to the bones, by developing the characters. Using previous exercises create histories for the characters, give them desires and drives, and invest them with contradictions and conflicts.

Part three – story model and issue
Participants: All groups, individual

In Chapter 3, we looked at 'issue': the aspect of a story that tackles a specific social/political/economic matter. What might be the issue(s) explored in this story? What research is suggested?

Example 88.4

In the example story outline, a clear issue would be the question of asylum and the situation of people seeking it.

Part four – story model and theme
Participants: All groups, individual

In Chapter 2, we looked at 'theme': the aspect of a story that addresses large, universal human concerns, often expressed in the abstract: loyalty, power, justice, revenge, etc. What might be the theme(s) explored in this story?

Example 88.5

In the example story outline, the themes of power/powerlessness would be expressed through the issue (the situation of asylum seekers in relation to the authority of the state).

Outcome

You now have a complete story outline that:

- Is event-driven.
- Has characters with drives, conflicts etc.
- Has a specific social issue that impacts on the lives of the characters.
- Has a major theme that springs from the issue.

SUMMARY

'Getting the story' is based upon:

- The development of a believable protagonist in a believable world, be it contemporary, historical, mythical, science-fictional, etc.

- The revelation of the true character of the protagonist through the choices they make under pressure.
- The progression of events by which the protagonist achieves/fails to achieve their conscious/unconscious goals.
- The arrival at an outcome/resolution which is appropriate to all the above.

Through Chapters 3, 4 and 5, you have become used to making constant revisions to the ongoing work. You will now – either as an individual writer or as a collaborative group – have begun to have a feel for the overall shape of the story you are writing, and the defined characters that inhabit the story. Give yourselves a deadline for completing a first draft. Those of us who are commissioned playwrights both dread and welcome deadlines. Welcome them because it means a payment on delivery, and dread them because it is a measure of commitment to a narrative that might seem flawed at this stage. But a deadline does no end of good to the creative spirit: you will find that the approaching date can produce a burst of energy that solves all sorts of problems you've been having with the script. After that you can review the whole text (testing it out again with many of the exercises you have done already) and take on board the work in Chapter 8: the second draft.

Before that, there are a couple of chapters focussing on two crucial aspects of your process. Chapter 6 will deal with the visualisation of the story – where it is located and how that impacts upon the narrative. Chapter 7 will deal with your own individual voice as a writer (or as a group of writers working collaboratively).

6 Location

If you are an individual writer or a collaborative/devising group writing for a conventional theatre-performance, you will be thinking about the location(s) that the story takes place in. There are many opinions about how much information and detail the writer needs to supply for the director, designer, lighting designer and sound-artist in order to realise the physical embodiment of the story. My own taste is to be minimal, and to allow as much scope to the other artists as possible. However I would suggest that, as you write, you do need to be as specific in your mind regarding the location(s) as you are with the characters. My own way of dealing with this is to 'think film', knowing that – in the end, and wonderfully so – the unique power of live performance can suggest a burning skyscraper through a burning matchstick.

Here are some of the ways that certain playwrights have given guidance to the production teams that will realise their work.

A section of the park on SORIN'S estate. A broad avenue leads away from the audience into the depths of the park towards the lake. The avenue is closed off by a stage which has been hurriedly run up for some home entertainment, so that the lake is completely invisible. Right and left of the stage is a shrubbery. A few chairs and a garden table.

The sun has just set. On the improvised stage, behind the lowered curtain, are YAKOV and other WORKMEN; coughing and banging can be heard. MASHA and MEDVEDENKO enter left, on their way back from a walk.

(*The Seagull*, by Anton Chekhov)

For Samuel Becket's *Waiting for Godot*, all we are told is: '*A country road. A tree. Evening.*'

In *The Sea*, by Edward Bond, we are presented with a physical world that is violently alive: '*Darkness and thunder. Wind roars, whines, crashes and screams over the water . . .*' *Masses of water swell up, rattle and churn, and crash back into the sea.*

It is useful to think of the location/setting of the drama as another character, not just as the incidental background. We have already talked about 'specificity': if you have a character who is a soldier on a battlefield, we need to know which particular soldier, on which particular battlefield, in which particular part of the battlefield. The war might be one that has never happened, a purely mythic event, but the details – however minimal – need to be as exact in your mind as they would be if you were writing a drama set in the trenches of World War I. This does not mean to say that we cannot be minimal in our descriptions, as long as they summon up a place that is, or seems, familiar.

Chekhov opens his play with a detailed description of a private estate in Russia in the late nineteenth century. It is our first glimpse of a world in which there are divisions of class (men who work in the grounds and people who go for walks in them), and of an event that will be taking place there (a stage being built). Beckett presents us with something much more minimal: a place, an object in the place, the time. We discover someone failing to take his shoe off. The very sparse information is as exact as Chekhov's. The fact that Beckett does not fill in the picture suggests that there is very little else in it: a landscape that has 'a tree' feels like a very bleak place, and such a place in the evening must be even bleaker.

Edward Bond presents us with more nature, in a violent image. Here, location-as-character is fully depicted. In the opening moments one of the characters is literally battling with it.

The English critic and dramaturge Kenneth Tynan once said, 'How I tire of settings that seek to represent nowhere-in-general: how I long to see everywhere-in-particular.' Minimal as it is, Beckett's landscape is particular to itself, but it could be anywhere in the world where a country road and a tree can be found at evening. It becomes universal by being particular. To broaden the description would have, in this case, limited it. Chekhov's detailed account of a particular country estate has echoes of such places that may be found anywhere in the world. If he had been less specific, it would have weakened the universality. Bond's tempest-tossed beach is the East Coast of England in 1907, with its gravel and sand, but will be familiar to anyone who has witnessed the power of the sea anywhere in the world.

LOCATION AS CHARACTER

Location and setting spell out certain 'rules', or conventions of behaviour, that will operate on the characters, just as they do in life. If I wish to declare my love for you, the environment we are in will dictate how I do it.

Exercise 89 A declaration of love
Participants: All groups, individual

1   Write the scene.

2   You are going to rewrite the scene, placing it in a particular location. The outcome will always be the same.

3   A library is a place that requires us to speak in hushed voices. Rewrite the scene in which the characters observe that constraint.

4   Rewrite the scene in which one or both of the characters break through the constraints of the location.

5   Rewrite the scene in any of the following locations: a crowded tube-train, a meadow, a funeral service, a cliff-top, a nightclub, a beach, a funfair, etc. In each case, explore how the location is an active participant in the event. You may find that the location begins to dictate a different outcome. If so, allow that to happen and follow it through.

Outcome

How does the location operate on the characters? How does it affect the way they speak, the words they use, the way they are with each other? The location is spelling out what is possible/allowable: telling someone you are in love with them in a funfair may be easier than at a funeral service – or not.

Exercise 90 If walls could speak
Participants: Primary

1   Think about your school: its age and history, what happens in it, the types of spaces in it, its surroundings, the sorts of people in it, etc. Think about what it is like at different times of the day and night. Make drawings of it. Take photographs of it.

2 Think of your school as a person. It can think, feel and speak. Like you it has different moods, memories and hopes, etc.

3 Using your research, write a speech for your school. Is it happy or sad? What does it feel about you? What are its good memories and its bad memories? (See Example 90.1.)

4 Write a scene where someone in the school is able to talk to it. No one else can do this, or knows about this. In the scene, the school is worried about something and is asking for advice. (See Example 90.2.)

5 In Example 90.1 the school took its revenge on the door-slammers by breaking the computers. Write a scene where the school gets involved in any of these: bullying, the Xmas play, racial harassment, sports day, community relations, etc.

6 Think of other places you know. What would they sound like if they could speak? What sort of things would they be interested in or want to get involved in?

Example 90.1

'Here they come again. Ouch! Don't slam that door. I've only just woken up. I had such a lovely sleep, I was dreaming about last Christmas, when everyone sang. Ouch! I wish you'd stop doing that. If you're not careful I'll have an illness, then all the electricity will go off, just like last month. Then your computers will break. Ha ha! That'll teach you. Ouch! Alright then . . . etc.'

Example 90.2

Person: Why are you sad today?
School: You were fighting in the classroom.
Person: So?
School: You chucked paint all over me. I hate red. I'm meant to be blue.
Person: It will get cleaned off, then you'll be blue again.
School: They won't bother. They never bother.
Person: Never mind.
School: Look at my outside, it's filthy. Why don't they make you all wash me down.
Person: Don't cry.
School: I'm not crying, it's my roof leaking. How would you like to have a leaky head?
Etc.

Outcome

By bringing a familiar location alive, the exercise invites the writers to think of 'the place the story happens in' as a character. It can intervene in events (making the electricity fail and breaking the computers), or comment on the behaviour of the 'real' characters (making a mess with paint, not bothering about the dirt). It also provides great opportunities for bringing social issues and research projects alive. The use of the location as a character allows difficult or contentious issues to be voiced in a safe way.

LOCATION AS STORY-EVENT

The location and what is happening to it, or in it, can provide the basis for a whole story, determining the actions of all the characters. The story of *The Titanic* is a perfect example: a ship hits an iceberg and sinks, and many people drown. There are many individual stories within the big event, but the major story and main character is the location itself. Here is an exercise that explores how what is happening to, or in, a location can impact on the lives of all the characters.

Exercise 91 On this day
Participants: All groups, individual

1   What you are going to write will take place in your locality or community. This could be a city, town, village, school, etc.

2   Think of a public event that happened in the locality or community. It will be an event that everyone in the locality or community will be aware of, even if they had not been directly involved in it. (See Examples 91.1.)

3   Everyone in the locality or community will have been affected by or involved in the event in any number of ways: physically, emotionally, economically, spiritually, etc. It will be something that everyone has some form of opinion about. The narratives you are going to write will all take place on the day of the event.

4   Draw a large circle. Inside it, draw nine concentric circles. They will get smaller and smaller, like onion-rings.

5   The smallest circle (C1), at the centre, is the event that took place. If your story takes place here, the characters will have been directly involved in the event in one way or another. If your story takes place on the largest circle (C10), the outer one, the lives of the characters

will have been marginally involved in the event. But even so, it will have had some effect on them, in some way.

6 The other circles (C2–C9) are all somewhere on the scale between 'directly involved' and 'marginally involved'.

7 Choose whereabouts on the scale of C1–C10 your story is set.

8 Decide upon a person who would have been in the location or community at the time of the event. Using all the work done so far, create a thumbnail back-story for them.

9 Decide where your protagonist is on the day of the event, and what they are doing. Where they are on the scale will suggest possibilities.

10 Bearing in mind where on the C1–C10 scale the protagonists are, write short outlines (two or three sentences) or beginnings of dramatic narratives. Try different points on the scale. (See Examples 91.2.)

11 Develop the scenario of one of the narratives. In terms of where the story is on the scale, does this begin to make things more complex? (See Example 91.3.)

12 Develop the scenario into scenes or a full play, depending upon the amount of time you have. How are the lives of the protagonists affected, changed, altered, shaped, hindered, etc., by the event?

13 Create (as an individual or a group) a sequence of short narratives placed 'on this day', giving a wide picture of how a whole locality or community was affected by the event.

Examples 91.1

These are some examples of location-events that were developed into narratives through workshops I have led:

- In London there was a huge storm, during which thousands of trees were blown down overnight. The city was reduced to chaos.
- In London a huge bomb, supposedly planted by the IRA in the Docklands, caused loss of life and huge damage.
- The day a member of the Royal Family came to the school.
- The day the city won the football cup.
- The day of the annual Mela (Asian festival).

Examples 91.2

- A tree has fallen on a young boy on his way to school. He is trapped underneath it. His parents have been located. Workers attempt to free him before another tree, directly above them, comes down (C1).

- An Irish barman in the City of London is serving customers. Overhearing anti-Irish talk, he attempts to adopt an English accent (C5).

- The owner of a flower-shop prepares bouquets. They are for children to give to the Queen (C7).

- While watching the football match, the sixteen-year-old boy receives a call on his mobile. His mother is ill in hospital. He has to choose whether to stay for the final score or go home (C3).

- While her friends go to the Mela, a young girl buries her pet dog (C10).

Example 91.3

The young girl has been preparing for the Mela for weeks. She and her friends have been practising traditional song, which they will perform at the event. That morning, her pet dog is run over by a car and dies. Her friends tell her that they will make a ceremony and bury the dog in the evening, but the girl does not want to delay it that long. Despite the persuasions of her friends, and her own desire to be at the Mela, she decides that she will remain alone. She questions the nature of loyalty, friendship and community. Although she is not now directly involved with the event (C10), her decision to not be a part of it has raised fundamental questions for her (C1).

Outcome

You have used the 'location-event' as a framing dramatic moment for the story. In doing so you have explored how the environment a story takes place in can be an active driving force, not just a background.

Exercise 92 The five places
Part one
Participants: All groups – drama activity into writing

1   Work individually at first. Find your own place in the room. Close your eyes for a few moments.

2   When you open your eyes you will be *on the top of a high mountain.* Look around you. What do you see? What is the temperature? What are you feeling? Don't attempt 'acting' or showing what you are thinking and feeling; keep the process very internal. Close your eyes.

3   When you open your eyes you will be *in a great meadow of grass.* Think of the questions. Close your eyes.

4   When you open your eyes you will be *in a dark forest.* Same process.

5   When you open your eyes you will be *on a busy street corner.* Same process.

6   When you open your eyes you will be *in a prison cell.* Same process.

7   Go through all the steps again. This time you can (a) sit, lie down, crouch, etc., depending on how you are feeling and (b) express your feelings in words each time you are in a new place.

8   Now work in groups of five.

9   Create a group tableau for each place, giving a strong physical feeling of the atmosphere, mood, etc. Add in all the words for each stage of the journey.

10 Write out the words for each stage of the journey. Decide on the order of the lines. How are they best put together to capture the feeling of each place?

Examples 92.1

Mountain:

·   Cold and high and flying.
·   Moon cold and long shadows in the valley.
·   Far, far away and so lonely.
·   I will never get home.
·   My feet on the edge.

Meadow:

·   Warm and the grass is new.
·   The grass sways in the breeze.
·   The long grass the soft grass.
·   I am safe.
·   I am sad.

Part two – the five places
Participants: All groups

1   Work either as a group or individually.

2   You now have five 'mood poems' for each place. Think of the journey from the top of the mountain to the prison cell. Decide who the person making this journey is.

3   The key episodes in the story are the five places. It is the influence of each place that leads the character to make decisions or take action. Write down what they are thinking, feeling and doing. Use the original words from the 'mood poems' as clues and inspiration. (See Examples 92.2.)

4   Write down what happens in between the five key episodes.

Examples 92.2

This is a fable (with overtones of Oedipus or prophet-from-the-wilderness stories) that one group of students came up with:

- He has come to the mountain to commit suicide, but the beauty of the view gives him a spiritual vision. He decides to go back to the world and spread that vision.

- In the meadow he falls asleep. The breeze in the grass seems to sing. It tells him that the people in the city on the other side of the forest need his vision. He decides to make his way to the city.

- Walking through the forest he loses his way. He has not eaten for days. With his last strength he climbs the tallest tree. From there he can see the way to the city. There is an eagle's nest in the tree. In the nest are some eggs. He eats the eggs, even though he knows he is robbing the mother of her children. The eagle returns as he does so and pecks out one of his eyes.

- On the street corner he preaches his message to the passers-by. It is hot and dusty and noisy. People push and shove at each other. Fights break out. No one listens to him. He starts to shout and scream. Still no one will listen. He points to his empty eye-socket. He says that he once did an evil thing and this was his punishment. He says that this will be their punishment if they do not mend their ways. The crowd turns on him and demands that he is arrested.

- In the prison cell he awaits his sentence. He uses a rusty nail to scratch on the wall the outline of the vision he had on the mountain. The guard tells him that he is to be imprisoned here for life. He kills himself with the nail.

Outcome

Through a simple drama/devising activity, it is possible to build a narrative that explores how location can impact on the journey of a character. In the example given, nature inspires the character, it advises him, it punishes him. The urban landscape ignores him, then turns on him. The place of confinement at the end leads him to escape the world, just as he had intended on the mountain.

Exercise 93 Mapping the locality

Participants: All groups – drama activity into writing

1   On separate sheets of paper write down, or draw, key locations in your area. Go for a good range and variety of public spaces and buildings, shops and markets, landmarks, etc.

2   Place these on the floor, making a map of the area.

3   Suggest types of characters who might be found in the area, where they could be and what they might be doing. These can be people you actually see in the area, and fictional characters. Give them an occupation or an activity in the area. (See Examples 93.1.)

4   Take a character and give them a 24-hour journey through the area. Where would they be at particular times? What would they be doing? Go for quite low-key, everyday activities, but remember that people can often have surprising aspects to them. (See Examples 93.2.)

5   Walk the characters through the floor map of the area. Where are they at certain times of the day? Which characters are at or near the same location at certain times of the day? How might they meet and what would occur at that meeting? Ask the characters to talk about their lives. Ask the characters questions. (See Examples 93.3.)

6   Give the characters the following: (a) a strong personal memory linked to a location in the area, (b) something like about the area, (c) something they dislike about the area. (See Examples 93.4.)

7   On the basis of steps 5 and 6, what possible dramatic narratives emerge? Try and relate them to the locations. (See Examples 93.5.)

8   See if the stories begin to link up with each other.

Examples 93.1

·   The young boy who is down-and-out on the steps of the tube station.

·   The French girl serving in the coffee bar.

·   The bored man behind the counter in the newsagent's.

·   The traffic warden who whistles.

·   The bald flower-seller on the corner.

·   Etc.

Examples 93.2

The traffic warden:

- 8.00: leaves her flat near the park.
- 9.00: working outside the town hall.
- 10.00: working along the high street.
- 11.00: has morning break in the coffee bar.
- 12.00: working outside the school.
- 13.00: goes to church to pray.
- Etc.

Examples 93.3

- 11.00: the traffic warden buys her coffee from the French girl.
- 14.00: the traffic warden gives the down-and-out young man fifty pence.
- 15.00: the down-and-out buys a bar of chocolate from the newsagent's.
- 16.00: the French girl buys some flowers from the stall on the corner.

Examples 93.4

The traffic warden:

- (Memory) The corner of the road, near the park, where her son was killed by a speeding car.
- (Likes) The park.
- (Dislikes) The litter.

The down-and out:

- (Memory) The music festival in the park last month.
- (Likes) The warm air that comes up from the tube station as he sits on the steps.
- (Dislikes) The litter.

Examples 93.5

- A traffic warden had a son who was killed by a speeding car. It happened at a corner near the park. A young man who is down-and-out and sits on the steps of the tube station reminds her of the son. She wants to rescue him.

- A French girl once had a date with an English boy. The first time they met, he bought her a red rose at the flower stall on the corner. He was run over by a car the next day. She knows his mother lives in the area, but does not know how to find her.

Outcome

In all narratives, the location is alive with possibilities: the impact of memory, necessity, chance, etc. Consider how – if you have a variety of locations in your play – these may operate on your characters. How differently do they behave in different locations?

7 The individual voice

'Afternoons seem unending on branch-line stations in England in summer time.'
(From *A Wreath of Roses*, by Elizabeth Taylor, first published by Richard Clay and Company, UK 1949)

The quote is not from a play, but is the opening line from a story by the English novelist Elizabeth Taylor. It is a fine example of how a writer can use words to cast a bright new light on the mundane and familiar. An examination of the phrase – the placing of the words, the rhythm of the words, the punctuation – shows that the author constructed it with as much care as the composer of a piece of music placing the notes on the page. A brief description of a moment in time, it has no internal punctuation but rolls itself out along a sequence of lazy, open vowels towards the final full stop. The placing of 'on', 'in' and 'in' add to the tangible sense of time going on forever. For me, it is one of those phrases that puts into words something I have experienced (waiting on a deserted country station in the hot summer for the train that never comes) in a manner that sums up the essence of that experience. The writer's individual voice, the value she placed on the words, gave verbal expression to a feeling I recognised, a thought I didn't know I had.

It must have been like that when people in sixteenth-century England heard – for the first time – thoughts uttered in speeches beginning with 'To be, or not to be, that is the question' and 'Tomorrow, and tomorrow, and tomorrow, creeps in this petty pace from day to day'. When Masha, in *The Seagull*, says 'I am in mourning for my life', she similarly expresses in words some intangible and melancholy feelings many of us have had at some time in our lives: the pointlessness of it all. When Noel Coward talks about the potency of cheap music, he is acknowledging the force with which a brilliant popular lyric can put into words something we have all felt, be it Edith

Piaf saying she regrets nothing or Frank Sinatra declaring he did it his way. It's the 'Ah yes' factor. 'Ah yes, that's *exactly* how it is.'

From the complex philosophical broodings of Shakespeare to the great modern lyricist, the individual writer can articulate for us our own thoughts and feelings. This must surely be the aspiration of anyone who puts pen to paper, or finger to keyboard: to capture in words a *personal* expression of thought or feeling that translates into a *universal* expression of the same. How?

This is the one aspect of writing that cannot be taught, and it is the most crucial one, without which all the questions of form and structure are hollow and mechanistic: how you discover your own individual voice through the way you use words. In this chapter I will be offering ways in which this aspect of the craft – if it cannot be 'taught' – can be encouraged.

In the play you are writing, you are creating a world that may seem familiar in its outward form (modern social drama, for example), or a new world that is unfamiliar in its outward form (historical, absurdist or futuristic drama, for example). Your task is to express the world you are depicting in a way that is unique to you, but which will re-create any of those worlds in a way that we believe in them utterly. None of them will be 'real'. The world of John Osborne's *Look Back In Anger* (Nottingham sweet-seller in the 1950s UK) is no more 'real' than Tennessee William's *Camino Real* (fictional literary characters trapped in an unnamed banana republic in the 1950s). What marks both plays out is their use of language. The language summons up the *essence* of the time/place of the story, but it is essentially the language of the poet. No one in Nottingham in the 1950s actually spoke like Jimmy Porter in Osborne's play. No one trapped in a banana republic in the 1950s would speak like Casanova in Tennessee William's play. What makes the plays great is that we *believe* that this is 'real'. That is what we must aspire to. If we do not, we might create a 'well-made play' crafted according to solid principles, but it will not be telling us anything new. It might make money, of course: Agatha Christie's *The Mousetrap* has been playing its wooden dialogue in London's West End for nearly as many years as I have been alive, and it only tells us who did the murder. There is no music in the language, or if there is, it is a very dull tune we have heard before.

LANGUAGE AS MUSIC

We have already talked about how any good actor will instinctively take to a script in which the placing of the words and the rhythms of the dialogue are fresh and original. They will be interested in plot, character-development, etc., but their actor's imagination will be primarily engaged with the words you have chosen for them to speak. You may be writing in a style that draws upon the language of the streets, or in a heightened poetic style. In either case the actor will know if you have placed value on the way you have laid the words down, or if the words are merely a vehicle to advance the plot. Actors will speak of the 'musicality' of the text and they are being very precise here, for they are talking about the exact placing of the words on the page (and therefore the weight given to them, and the punctuation). Before engaging in any practical writing work, it will be useful to take some proven plays and see what we make of this.

Exercise 94 The placing of the word
Participants: All groups, individual

This is an exercise which actors and directors often use at the start of rehearsals, as part of the process of getting to grips with a text. It is not about character-development, etc., but more an examination of the poetics of the text. For writers it is equally useful as a means of experiencing how a skilled practitioner has chosen to lay out the words in a specific way.

1   Select a passage from the opening scene of any act in a play. It should preferably be one that is not known to you or to the group, so that there will be no preconceptions about it. (See Example 94.1.)
2   You are going to read through the passage.
3   Put aside any questions of who the characters are or what the story is.
4   Read the passage as a series of speeches unrelated to character. If you are working in a group read speech-by-speech around the circle. (See Example 94.2.)
5   Read the passage again. This time, read it as a series of thoughts. That is, each thought ends with the full stop. Again, if working in a group, read thought-by-thought around the circle. (See Example 94.3.)
6   Read through the passage. Draw a circle around all the major words or phrases that appear more than once, or words that belong in similar categories. Read them out giving each one its full weight. (See Example 94.4.)
7   Take a scene from your own play and apply the same process to it.

Example 94.1

An opening scene
The SKIPPER, in a small pool of light. He has a small, battered tin globe, with all the time zones, meridians, etc., on it. He spins it. The OWNER enters.
Skipper: (pointing to the small, battered globe) Put your finger down, anywhere.

Bet your bottom dollar I've been there.
(He spins the globe. The OWNER puts his finger down)
Been there. Cancer, Capricorn, Equator, parallel. I've seen the lot.

Owner:	Safe home in harbour now.
Skipper:	I'm not worn out yet. Nor me, nor boat.
Owner:	She's pooped.
Skipper:	My boat?
Owner:	My boat.
Skipper:	Yours by property, mine by feeling.
Owner:	Time's up for that old tub.
Skipper:	No...never.
Owner:	The firm recognises all you've done...(hands him a package) You'll have a tidy pension, too.

(The SKIPPER takes out a watch and chain from the package)
We're calling her in.

Skipper:	And me? I'm to tick off my days?
Owner:	Her time's up.
Skipper:	She's not a boating-lake dinghy, with a ticket and a number...
Owner:	Woodwork's all gone to pot...
Skipper:	A bit of care...:
Owner:	Brasswork comes off in your hand...
Skipper:	Bit of love and affection...
Owner:	Money's tight. Her days are done.
Skipper:	Like me?
Owner:	You'd never manage the new ships.
Skipper:	I've seen them. That's not ships. That's floating factories, floating coffins.
Owner:	That's the modern world. Brass and wood is history. Come round next month. You can supervise the breaking up.
Skipper:	Break her?
Owner:	Strip her to the bone, sell off her parts. You'll get a bonus.
Skipper:	Just one last sailing...
Owner:	Out of the question...
Skipper:	A short trip...anything.
Owner:	I might be owner, but I've shareholders to answer to. No. She's had her day. She's done. You too.

Example 94.2

Reader One:	Put your finger down, anywhere. Bet your bottom dollar I've been there. Been there. Cancer, Capricorn, Equator, parallel. I've seen the lot.
Reader Two:	Safe home in harbour now.

Reader Three: I'm not worn out yet. Nor me, nor boat.
Reader Four: She's pooped.
                Etc.

Example 94.3

Reader One: Put your finger down, anywhere.
Reader Two: Bet your bottom dollar I've been there.
Reader Three: Been there.
Reader Four: Cancer, Capricorn, Equator, parallel, I've seen the lot.
Reader Five: Safe home in harbour now.
                Etc.

Example 94.4

Dollar. Cancer. Capricorn. Equator. Parallel. Home. Harbour. Worn out. Boat. Pooped. Boat. Boat. Property. Feeling. Old tub. Pension. Tick. Time. Etc.

Outcome

At first glance, the passage might seem to be a casual, 'realistic' exchange. But when we strip away the layers, we discover there is a sequence of key 'notes' being struck, embedded in an overall 'score'. The passage has been composed.

Actors who perform in Shakespeare will tell you that, if you respect the punctuation, you are halfway there. The 'meaning' of the text resides as much in the shape of the verse (its musicality), as in the intellectual dissection of the thought behind it.

Exercise 95 The sound of the word

Participants: All groups, individual

The words you choose to put into the mouths of your characters convey much more than information. Their very sound and shape might begin to summon up the mood and atmosphere of the play, the situation of the moment and even character-type. The choice of hard/soft sounds, vowels/consonants, short/long words.

1   Take some passages or scenes from different plays.
2   Note the location.
3   Note what the main action is.

4   Note what you identify as the mood/atmosphere of the passage or scene.

5   See if the types of words used – in their sound and structure – reflect in any way steps 2, 3 or 4.

6   See if the types of words used give an impression of the characters, what type of person they might be or what emotional state they are in at the moment.

Example 95.1 *The Sea*, by Edward Bond

The opening scene of this play is set on a beach; there is darkness, thunder and a violent storm. The main action is the failure of one of the characters to rescue his friend from the water. The atmosphere is one of great confusion. Two characters, WILLY and EVANS speak over the tempest. WILLY is attempting to save someone from the sea. EVANS is drunk. Throughout the scene, WILLY uses words that tend to be short, hard and forceful: help, shout, god, water, boat, bastard, etc. EVANS uses words that are short, soft and weak: sing'ss, song, day'ss, wha'?, 'ssea'sl, thass, wasser. The language being used therefore has more than one function. It tells us that WILLY is desperate and angry and that EVANS is drunk and bewildered; but beyond this the very sounds of the words mirror the elements the men are thrown into: the violence of the storm.

Outcome

We have seen that characters in a play, as in life, can express their inner-selves by the words they use. It is no coincidence that ugly, aggressive insult words often begin with hard or plosive consonants: F, C, B, D, etc. 'Sad' and 'melancholy' have downward inflections, and a person in such a state of mind may well use words that have a similar ring: 'if only', lonely', 'hopeless', etc. Your task as the writer is to choose those words that will reflect the character's inner-state, and give resonance to the mood and atmosphere of the scene. We will explore this further later on in the chapter.

Exercise 96 The essence of the word
Part one
Participants: All groups, individual

1   Write down a list of feelings or emotions: Anger, Grief, Forgiveness, Hatred etc.

2   Choose one of the words. Write a list of words or phrases that come to mind when you think of the word. Try for about twelve words or phrases. Don't mention the actual word itself. (See Example 96.1.)

3   If you are working as a group, read out the individual lists. See if the rest of the group can identify the feeling or emotion each list is describing.

4   From the list, identify five single words. They are the ones that, for you, most strongly give a sense of the feeling or emotion: the essence of the original word. (See Example 96.2.)

5   Using the five words only, create a monologue or poem that expresses the essence of the original word. Play with the five words, creating patterns of sound with them. Do not go for logical 'sense'. You do not have to use all the words. You may find that some words have a stronger presence than others. Allow your intuition to guide you. (See Examples 96.3.)

6   Use the exercise to find the essence of other groups of words: the four elements, the seven deadly sins, the four seasons, life-passage (birth, death), etc.

Example 96.1

Anger:

•   Hot.

•   Boiling up.

•   Screaming at me.

•   Like a clenched fist.

•   Spitting out the words.

•   Cold and hard.

•   Like a war inside me.

•   Shout.

•   Letting it out.

•   Frustration.

•   When I'm told what to do.

Example 96.2

Anger: Cold. Boiling. Screaming. Out. Shout.

Examples 96.3

Anger

Cold cold cold out

Shout out shout out shout

Screaming

Screaming

Shout

Out out shout out

Out boiling boiling boiling

Jealousy: twisted, agony, gut-churning, revenge, irrational

Agony

Twisted agony

Gut-churning twisted agony

Irrational, irrational

Agony

Twisted agony

Gut-churning twisted agony

Irrational

Agony

Agony

Twisted agony

Gut-churning twisted agony

Irrational

Agony, agony, agony, agony

Twisted agony, twisted agony

Gut-churning, gut-churning

Gut churning twisted agony

Gut-churning twisted agony

(Pause)

Revenge

Outcome

By imposing the strict limitation of the number of words, you have created the 'essence' of an emotion or feeling. There is no hint of naturalism in the description, yet it probably has more dramatic power than if I had simply asked you to describe what 'anger' or 'jealousy' is. You have created a piece of heightened speech that could also be the basis of a passage of choral speaking, or a song.

Part two – the essence of the word
Participants: All groups, individual

1   Take two of the 'emotion monologues', preferably ones that are at opposite ends of the spectrum of emotions, for example 'love–hate', 'rage–compassion'.

2   Using the five 'essential' words for each emotion, create a dialogue for two voices.

3   Do not attempt to impose logical 'meaning' on the exchange; as in the previous exercise you are seeking the rhythms and patterns that your intuition suggests. Again, you do not have to use all the words, and you may find that some words have a stronger presence than others. (See Example 96.4.)

4   What images does the exchange suggest? What mood or atmosphere is conjured up. If you are working in a group, create dramatic images or tableaux that bring the exchange to life. (See Example 96.5.)

Example 96.4

Rage: war, prejudice, hate, powerlessness, nature

and

Compassion: orange, peace, solid, floating, cashmere

One: Hate, hate, hate.
Two: Peace.
One: Hate.
Two: Solid, solid.
One: Powerlessness.
Two: Orange.
One: Orange.
Two: Floating orange.
One: Peace, peace.

Two:	Powerlessness, powerlessness.
One:	Nature floating orange.
Two:	War floating nature.
One:	Hate, hate, hate.
Two:	Solid, solid.
Both:	Peace, peace, floating.

Example 96.5

In the group that produced the 'rage–compassion' dialogue, some of the first responses were like a dialogue happening between two sides of a single brain: one side wanting to calm the other down, the other side resisting. Someone suggested that 'orange' symbolised Buddhism and the peace movement. Someone else suggested the image of the 1960s' 'flower-power' movement, when anti-Vietnam war protesters placed flowers in the barrels of soldiers' guns. Two members of the group created the physical image. Two other members of the group spoke the words. What had seemed on paper to be an exchange of words that was abstract to the point of having no meaning at all, suddenly came alive as a powerful expression of a conflict: the rigidity of power versus the need to change. It was noted that this was achieved through a use of words that was entirely poetic and abstract; no 'opinion' or 'logical argument' had been expressed and the moment was the more powerful because of that. It was a good example of how a big public 'issue' can be addressed through poetry as opposed to polemic: we will be looking further at this in Chapter 8.

Outcome

From a very simple exercise exploring the essence of single emotions, you have created the basis for a dramatic moment. You have explored how 'meaning' is something that does not have to be imposed, but can be discovered by allowing our mind to operate intuitively. If you have been working in a group, you have seen how the 'meanings' drawn from a written passage may be as various as the number of people listening to it. The two writers who made the 'rage–compassion' exchange had not been thinking about the Vietnam, Buddhists or flowers, but these were images the piece had stimulated in the minds of the listeners.

LANGUAGE AS ESSENCE

The novelist Elizabeth Taylor captured the *essence* of waiting on the empty platform for the train that never comes. She did this through the poetry of her language. This is what live drama can do: give us an essence of the human experience, boiled down to Shakespeare's 'two hours traffic on the stage'.

The following exercises explore how our own use of the written word can throw a new light on the familiar.

Exercise 97 Letter to the Alien

Participants: All groups (30–60 minutes)

For this exercise you will need 26 large sheets of paper (flipchart size) and enough black felt markers for the whole group.

1 This is a preparation task. At the top of the first sheet of paper write the letter A. At the top of the second sheet write the letter B, and so on. You will have the 26 letters of the alphabet on the 26 sheets. Now put these aside for the moment.

2 Turn to a clean page in your notebook. Draw a margin down the left-hand side of the page.

3 Down the margin write the letters of the alphabet: A at the top of the column, Z at the bottom.

4 Imagine that an Alien is going to visit us in an hour's time. The Alien knows nothing about our world, and your task will be to introduce her to it.

5 You are going to write down a list of 26 single words. Each word will represent something you feel will be useful for the Alien to know about. They can be feelings and emotions, objects (animal, vegetable, mineral; natural or human-made), colours, institutions, places, activities, etc. They might be things of danger that the Alien should be aware of, things she would need, things you would like to share with her, etc.

6 The first word on the list will start with A, the second with B, and so on down to the last, which will start with Z. (See Example 97.1.)

7 When it comes to the letters X and Z you can break the rule: the letter can appear anywhere in the word. (See Example 97.2.)

8 Don't think too hard. If you get stuck on a letter, skip to the next and go back later. This should take about 5–10 minutes at the most.

9 Everyone in the group will now have their own list of things they want the Alien to know about.

10 Now lay out all the large paper sheets in a circle, in alphabetical order. The circle will start with A and end with Z. The circle can be either on

the floor or on tables. It is important that the sheets are not crowded and that there is room to move around the outside of the circle.

11   With your notebook and a black marker, take a place on the circle, next to any of the letters. The group should spread itself evenly around the circle.

12   Look at the large sheet and the letter at the top of it. From your notebook, transfer the word that starts with that letter to the sheet. Write the word in capitals, so that everyone can read it.

13   You can use words that are not English, as long as you give the translation.

14   Proceed to the next sheet of paper (everyone moving in the same direction), adding the next word under the letter at the top.

15   As the lists of words collect, keep them as a list down the page.

16   If you come to a sheet on which someone else has written the same word as you have for that letter, still write yours down.

17   By the end you will be back at the letter you started with, having visited every sheet of paper and transferred all the words from your notebook.

18   There will now be a list of words on each of the 26 large sheets (all the A-words on the A-sheet, all the B-words on the B-sheet, etc.). (See Example 97.3.)

19   The number of words on each sheet will be the same as the number in the group (give or take a few blanks in people's lists). Take one of the sheets near you.

20   The Alien, who we were expecting, is not able to come just now. But she would love to hear from us. Your task is to write a letter to her, in which you will talk about the world you live in. Like any letter, it will be your own very personal view of the world: friendly, informal, informative.

21   Look at the large sheet of paper you have, with its list of words. The letter you write to the Alien will contain all those words, and they will appear in *exactly the same order* as they appear on the sheet. They will be the 'spine' of what you write, and your task is to find the manner in which the letter links them together.

22   Before you start, remember the advice for some of the earlier exercises: don't think too hard, don't attempt to 'plan', trust the words to pull you through. Above all, don't judge what you are writing. Go. (See Example 97.4.)

Example 97.1 Alphabet-word list

A.   Anger.
B.   Blue.

C. Christmas.
D. Death.
E. Elephants.
F. Factories.
G. Grandmothers.
H. Hope.
   Etc.

Example 97.2 X and Z

X. Excellence.
Y. Yellow.
Z. Lazy.

Example 97.3 First-letter lists

A	Z
Art	Zeichen (sign)
Animals	Cazar (hunt)
Androgyny	Ozone
Angst	Zion
Animals	Jazz
Aim	Horizon
Allah	Horizon
Art	Zest
Antiquity	Zen
Affection	Zen
Azure	Zanthe
Art	Zealous
Art	Zuizata (animals)
Art	Zip
Apartheid	Zap
AIDA	Zupped
Annie Lennox	Booze
Artistic	A–Z
Ability	Zoo
Atom	Frozen
Art	Zest
Anger	Zoo
Attention	
Apprehension	
Art	
Afraid	
Abstract	
Animals	

Example 97.4 Extracts from two letters to the Alien

(*Alphabet letter 'a'*)

Dear Alien

Art is unique to humans and is not, to our knowledge, practised by animals. It can be practised by males, females, or even as an expression of androgyny. It can express angst, such as fear of animals, or any number of other emotions – the aim being to affect the viewer and/or praise a deity such as Allah. Those art objects of antiquity are met with great affection, such as the azure Gainsborough painting the Blue Boy.

There is art for the sake of art as well as art in protest of something, such as apartheid, or in support of something, like those with AIDS. Annie Lennox has made quite a bit of money with her artistic ability. The enemy of art is the Atomska Bomba, which would remove all evidence, memory and existence of all pieces of art and those that appreciate them. This would happen under a circumstance of severe anger. The threat of the use of such a device is used to gain attention, but it is met with apprehension by nearly everyone. Art is a refuge for those who are afraid, and even abstract expressionism can lend strength, courage and enjoyment – as can animals.

(*Alphabet letter 'z'*)

Dear Alien

There is every zeichen (sign) we won't be around for much longer, what with the cazar (hunt) to preserve the ozone layer, I guess we'll never achieve our own particular Zion. In London, Zebra crossings are very dangerous and crap jazz resonates from horizon to horizon. Instead of zest, people turn to Zen. Though Zen again, Zanthe is still zealous. Zuizata (animals) are not having a good time. As for us, half of us are really zip-zap-zupped with the booze; the other half are zealots using the bible as an A–Z map for life. What a zoo! We're emotionally frozen. Where's the zest? 'Zoo' long!

Outcome

By imposing the restriction of the list on the task of explaining our world to the Alien, the writer is liberated into a new, imaginative territory. The 'limitation that stimulates' demands that links be made between things that seem to have no relation to each other. If I had just set the task of writing a letter about our world to the Alien, the results would probably have been quite earnest and essay-like, lacking the often quirky but telling imagery that the exercise encourages. It is another example of how, through words, we can throw a new light on the familiar; put things into new relations with each other. I have collections of letters to an Alien from all over the world, written by vastly different groups of people, and all of them contain phrases and images that sparkle. I will never forget: 'Education is dead and so are lots of elephants.'

Exercise 98 The five senses

Participants: All groups, individual (30–40 minutes)

1 Write a description of the room you are in. Make it as full as you can.

2 Think of someone you know. I have never met them. Imagine that this person will be at the same party as myself tonight. You won't be there, but you'd like me to meet them. Write a brief description of that person so that I would recognise them. (See Example 98.1.)

3 Draw five columns in your notebook. At the top of the columns write down the names of the five senses: Sight, Sound, Touch, Taste, Smell. In the columns, write down lists of words that can be used to describe all the senses. Make the lists as full as possible. (See Example 98.2.)

4 Now write a full description of the same person. This time, imagine that I was born without the sense of sight. You can use all the other senses but that one. (See Example 98.3.)

5 Now re-write the description of the room you are in, again without using the sense of sight: the sounds within it, the textures, the temperatures, the smells, the tastes. What is its atmosphere?

Example 98.1 Description of a stranger (a)

Dorothy is white and in her 80s. She has grey hair, with a little bit of a brown tint in it. She is about five foot four inches in height and is a little plump around the middle. She will be wearing quite conventional clothes, probably a skirt (knee-length) and a blouse. Bright colours, but nothing flashy. Flat shoes. She has a very open and warm smile. She might look a bit shy if there are lots of strangers, but once you say hello she'll be very friendly. She chuckles a lot. Quite a high pitched voice. She's a bit hard of hearing.

Example 98.2 Description of the senses

Sight	Sound	Touch	Smell	Taste
Colour	Resonance	Texture	Strength	Texture
Shape	Tone	Sensation	Quality	Quality
Size	Volume	Temperature	Memory	Temperature
Etc.	Etc.	Etc.	Etc.	Etc.

Example 98.3 Description of a stranger (b)

Dorothy is a bit hard of hearing, so you will have to speak clearly. When she speaks you will recognise her by a rather sing-song tone, quite light and sometimes a bit high-pitched (she has a habit of talking till she is out of breath and the ends of her sentences get a bit strangled). She wheezes a bit, because of her asthma, and has a bit of a lisp, which is probably to do with wearing false teeth. She will sound a bit shy (almost wary of you) at first, but once you get talking you will find her very warm and friendly and a bit girlish, despite her years. Once she feels comfortable with you she'll probably be saying 'my dear' to you, and she'll probably put her hand on your arm – it'll feel a bit claw-like, but that's because of her arthritis and it's a friendly gesture. She'll have some perfume on (even though she has no sense of smell herself, since childhood) and it'll be lily-of-the-valley (a clean, brisk scent), and you'll probably get a whiff of face-powder – a sort of dusty, old-fashioned smell. If you were to put your arm around her you'd feel that her back has a very slight hunch to it, due to her age. She'll be wearing a cotton blouse, possibly with a light-weight woollen cardigan over it. If you shake her hand she'll hang onto yours (you'll feel those little arthritic bumps and some of the fingers a bit bent). A general impression is one of a young girl in an old body, and you'll hear this in her voice, which can be all chuckles one moment and a bit mournful the next. I think she'd taste like the wrapped toffees she likes to eat (she'll probably offer you one).

Outcome

When we are asked to describe something, we tend to go primarily for the visual – that is, the outward appearance. By imposing the limitation of taking away the visual, we are actually liberating the use of the other senses, and from this emerges a stronger impression and imagery – an essence of the place or the person. The exercise is another reminder that, in seeking to develop our individual voice, we must strive to work against what seems to 'come naturally', when that can often mean taking the easy route.

This last exercise came out of working with a group of people involved in the disability-arts world. One member had been without sight since birth. I was talking to him one day and the conversation came around to the ways we describe things. He asked me to describe the room we were in, and of course I started in with colours, dimensions, etc., until I realised that this meant nothing to him. I asked him to describe the room and he did so, and it was stunning to realise that his so-called 'disability' actually equipped him with a far wider range of expression than my own. He stood in different parts of the room and described minute changes in temperature, movements of air, qualities of smell; he drew my attention to the many and varied sounds in the room, their tones and pitches; he detailed the textures of floor, walls and furnishings. All of this captured the essence of the room so much more effectively than my own ('It's about thirty feet square and its walls are black...etc.'). This is not to romanticise being blind, nor is the exercise intended to be about 'finding out what it's like to be blind'. But it is useful to realise that ways of being descriptive which seem to 'come naturally' to those of us who are sight-led might be a disability in itself.

LANGUAGE AND FEELING

In Exercises 94–98, we looked at how the words and phrases used can express – through their rhythms and musicality – underlying character and feeling. If the writer has placed these well, there will be no need to put in directions such as: *(Angrily)* or *(With great passion)* etc. There is feeling there, of course, and the actors will find their way to it if they trust the clues that are there in the way the text is laid out. Take any of the terse exchanges in a play by Harold Pinter, and see how there is a *pressure* on the language, and that pressure is the unspoken feelings. Rage, disdain and fear may all be there, but they are held in by the seemingly mild exchange of dialogue. So the writer's discovery of their own individual voice – particularly when writing plays – might take on board the possibility of resisting a display of full-on emotion. Let it bubble away under the surface. Hold your fire.

Exercise 99 A time in my life when...
Part one
Participants: All groups, individual

1   Think of a time in your life when you were in a very negative emotional place – unhappy, lonely, confused, etc.

2   Think of a room you were in at that time.

3   Place yourself back in that room.

4   Allow yourself the feelings or emotions you were experiencing at that time. Keep them at the front of your mind.

5   Write a description of the room. Be as detailed as possible. Keep it absolutely to the externals. *Do not describe the feelings or emotions.*

Part two – a time in my life when...
Participants: All groups, individual

1   Think of a moment/event in your life when you were in a very positive emotional place – happy, joyful, excited, contented, etc.
2   Remember where you were when this was happening.
3   Place yourself back in that moment.
4   Allow yourself the feelings or emotions you were experiencing at the time. Keep them at the front of your mind.
5   Write a description of what was happening. Be as detailed as possible. Keep it absolutely to the externals. *Do not describe the feelings or emotions.*

Outcome

By resisting any direct expression of what you were feeling at the time, but keeping those feelings at the front of your mind, you will have experienced how the pressure of the feelings have shaped the words you have written.

In the play you are writing you may well have moments where the characters are expressing their emotions full-tilt, and I am not suggesting this is wrong. What I am suggesting is that the task of 'finding your own voice' (and therefore the voices of the characters you are creating) might be as much about what is not said as what is said.

A final note regarding this exercise. It requests a possible level of self-revelation. My advice, if you are working in a group, is that it is made very clear that the results of this exercise do not necessarily have to be shared. Painful or potentially exposing situations may have been explored and the writer must be allowed to do this without self-censorship.

YOUR VOICE THEIR LANGUAGE

I have just mentioned 'the characters you are creating'. In fiction, as in life, every individual has their distinctive manner of speech: the rhythms, the patterns, the words and the phrases that mark them out. The development of your voice as a playwright must include the ability to develop the different voices of your characters. If the creation of a character in a drama is about being able to step into someone else's shoes, it is also therefore about being able to hear their voice and capture it in words. Here are a few exercises that explore different speech-patterns.

Exercise 100 Speech patterns
Part one
Participants: All groups, individual

You are going to write a series of short monologues for a range of different people. All the monologues will be on the theme of 'love'.

1   This person is very precise. She always finishing her thoughts. Very clear. Lots of full stops. I hope you get my meaning. I think it is important to be exact.

2   This person is so keen to make herself heard that she hardly ever gives herself time for a full stop ever well she'll go on and on until she's nearly strangled herself and even then she'll try and keep going and going until the breath runs out...

3   This person is very... imprecise and she... has... no, she has... many unfinished thoughts and lots of... lots of... well she's just the sort of person who...

4   This person cannot stick to the point. She has something she wants to explain/describe, but is (and of course this, came up when I was talking to you earlier, you will remember that I spoke of something similar, which reminds me...) constantly veering off into related subjects, which reminds me of the time when...

5   This person has a great tendency to frame her thoughts as questions. Don't you know the sort of person I'm talking about? Am I right? I wonder if you remember if this came up earlier in the book? Or did it?

6   This person always utilises grandiloquent and impressive words when small and exact ones would do. Am I validated here or am I right?

7   This person is always quoting, 'As the poet once said', from books, poems, plays, etc.

8   This person actually has a word or a phrase that actually constantly peppers her dialogue, actually.

9   This person is always apologising, if you don't mind me saying this, for what they are saying. I hope I've not offended you.

Part two – speech patterns
Participants: All groups, individual

1 Put any two of the characters above together.
2 Place them in a restaurant.
3 They are having a dialogue about what food to order.

Part three – speech patterns
Participants: All groups, individual

You are going to write a series of short monologues on the subject of 'war'.

1 This person talks like a tidal wave.
2 This person talks like a village pond.
3 This person talks like a stampede of horses.
4 This person talks like snake sliding through the grass.
5 This person talks like a nuclear explosion.
6 This person talks like a yapping dog.
7 This person talks like a meandering river.
8 This person talks like an army tank.
9 This person talks like a plodding carthorse.
10 This person talks at you.
11 This person talks to you.

Part four – speech patterns
Participants: All groups, individual

Put any three of the above together. They are at home. They are opening Christmas presents.

Exercise 101 Punctuation and rhythm
Participants: All groups, individual

Here is a speech without words. I will insert a _____ for every word and I will give the punctuation. Your task is to fill in the blanks. Don't worry if it doesn't make logical 'sense'. Don't think too hard about the words you are using – in fact you may find that you continue to use a small number of words in different ways.

Speech: ____ ____, ____ ____ ____ ____, ____ ____ ____? ____?
____ ____ ____ ____ ____ ... ____ ____ ____. ____ ____ ____ ____!
____ ____ ____ ____. ____. ____. ____ ____ ____ ____ ... ____
____ ____, ____ ____, ____ ____. ____!

Example 101.1

Oh yes, what a mess here, who did this? Well? Oh yes I can see...I can see. See what I'm seeing! I don't believe it. No. No. I just don't believe... It's a mess. A mess. Oh yes. Mess!

Outcome

With all the above exercises, we have seen that punctuation is not just an afterthought to the words. You could say that the way we think is the way that we punctuate our thoughts. So too with the characters we are writing. We have also begun to explore how the *types* of words a character uses tells us much.

Exercise 102 Your characters and their patterns
Participants: All groups, individual

Go back to any of the work you have done on your own play so far. See what characteristics and mannerisms mark out the different speech patterns. Take a scene or a passage of dialogue. Push the speech patterns to their limit.

Exercise 103 Language and gender
Participants: All groups, individual

1   Write a short scene for three characters (mixed gender). Name the characters. They have just been shoplifting. In the writing of the dialogue, push it as far as you can into male/female stereotype speech – that is, words that might be *associated* with a gender.

2   Write a short scene for three new characters (mixed gender). They are in a night-club. This time you are not going to reveal the gender. Impose the following limitations:

- do not reveal in any way the genders of the characters through types of words that may be associated with gender.
- name the characters by choosing nicknames that are gender-free.
- do not use 'her', 'him', 'she', 'he', etc.

Outcome

Writing 'the stereotype' comes easily, probably because it is all around us all the time in popular culture, the press, etc.: the stereotype 'teenage yob', 'tart-with-a-heart', 'harassed mother', etc. Our task as writers is to avoid the tired and easy way out ('that's how yobs speak') and find new ways of expressing those characters through language. We might be writing about a teenager who is expressing himself in an antisocial manner, or a racist expressing his extreme views, or a middle-class do-gooder patronising the poor; but if we simply resort to how they are popularly imagined to speak then we are not doing our jobs. We are simply parroting what we hear on the TV soaps.

THE POETRY OF THE EVERYDAY

TV soaps can deliver terrific story lines, great characters (particularly the female ones) and, occasionally, moments of true human insight. They popularise and make accessible social issues, sometimes honourably and sometimes sensationally. They are not, however, the arena in which spoken language (the vehicle of thought) is renewed and reinvigorated. The language in the soaps is rooted in a version of what is 'really' heard on the block. The characters use turns of phrase that we can hear in the pub, at the supermarket, down the club, but in a somewhat muted and sanitised way – no vigorous filthy language, no flights of fancy. The language of the everyday is rich and vibrant and should be celebrated. But it should also be challenged, developed and enriched. That is what playwrights can – must – do. And they can do it best in the medium of live theatre. As theatre-poets, you must not look down on or despise what is 'out there' in terms of the ways that people express their thoughts, feelings and desires in words. Take what is there and push it a little: I am sure that is what Shakespeare was doing, and what Brecht advised us to do.

Exercise 104 Street, pub, playground

Participants: All groups, individual (15–20 minutes)

1 Write down a list of everyday 'sayings', proverbs, turns-of-phrase. Go for about eight or nine. (See Examples 104.1.)

2 You are going to write a monologue. S/he has fallen in love.

3 The only words and phrases you can use are the ones in the list you made in step 1. You can use them any number of times and in any different combinations. (See Examples 104.2.)

4 Write monologues in which s/he is:

- Accepting an Oscar.
- Saying goodbye to her parents.
- Pleading in a courtroom for her life.
- Being bossy to her younger brother.

5 Take one of the characters from the play you are writing and apply the exercise to them.

6 Take a notebook out with you. Listen to conversations on the bus, in the shop, etc. What turns of speech are people using? Jot them down and use them.

Examples 104.1

- The lights are on but there's no one at home.
- She's no better than she should be.
- That's wicked that is.
- That's the truth.
- From the back of beyond.
- You must be joking.
- He was three sheets to the wind.
- I gave him a bunch of fives.

Examples 104.2

No one, no one, no one. Home...no better...the lights...she's...no better. That's wicked. Three sheets. She's...three sheets. That's wicked. Beyond wicked. Three sheets to the wind. Wicked. She's at home. The lights are on. Wicked, that is, wicked...etc.

Outcome

You have explored how 'common coinage' words and phrases can be a source of inspiration. You have used the 'limitation' of popular language as stimulation for your imagination. You have further developed the possibilities of non-naturalistic language.

THE STRUGGLE FOR ARTICULACY

How all occasions do inform against me,
And spur my dull revenge! What is a man,
If his chief good and market of his time
Be but to sleep and feed? A beast, no more.
Sure, he that made us with such large discourse, *   [Intelligence]*
Looking before and after, gave us not
That capability and god-like reason
To fust* in us unused.   [Grow mouldy, rot]*

(Hamlet, Act IV, Scene 4)

In developing the poetics of the language your characters are speaking, bear this in mind: all human beings desire to be understood, and desire to understand their own thoughts. Generally, we don't do a good job of it, and the English language is littered with the evidence:

- I just don't get it.
- I don't understand why I said that.
- I don't get your drift.
- I can't fathom her.
- I can't believe my ears.
- I'm not making any sense am I?
- I can't explain.
- Do you get my meaning?
- You haven't listened to a single word I've said.
- Words fail me.
  [Add to the list]

By 'struggling to be understood' I mean the struggle to articulate our thoughts and feelings exactly, through the vocabulary at our disposal. This does not always mean 'telling the truth', of course. There are situations where we use sophisticated tactics to cover up. We lie, dissemble, prevaricate, pretend not to have heard, deliberately mislead, etc. Many a good drama has been made from the basis of the clever killer's alibi versus the clever detective's outwitting of him. Hamlet – one of the most articulate fictional creations – spends the play (a) failing to understand his own nature, and (b) successfully fooling everyone else into thinking he is mad. In fact, the key to most dramas can be seen as the battle against the *failure to articulate*. Or perhaps, the *struggle to be understood*.

The characters in your play all have their own individual voices; which are of course different versions of your own individual voice. In earlier chapters we have explored ways of arriving at this differentiation. Here, I am suggesting that underlying everything is the struggle for articulacy and the *different levels it is operating on*. All of your characters have thoughts; the struggle to articulate them forms the poetics of their speech and the dynamic of the story.

Exercise 105 Levels of articulation
Participants: All groups, individual

Write the following scenes. Your point of focus is the attempt made by all the characters to express themselves to their advantage. Do they succeed? Do they fail? What is the *pressure of emotions* on the words they use?

1   A parent returns home from a business trip. They have left their sixteen-year-old son in charge of the house. The house is a wreck. The parent is *attempting to get to the bottom of things*. The son is *attempting to wriggle out of the situation*.

2   Over the phone, a father is *failing to describe* his feelings of love for his son.

3   A shop assistant, wishing to sell a pair of shoes, is *bombarding with information* a customer who is *trying to explain he doesn't really want to know*.

4   A doctor is *very cautiously approaching* the news of a life-threatening illness to a patient who *doesn't want to hear*.

5   A police officer tells a mother that her daughter has been killed in a road accident. The mother *refuses to hear* the news. The officer *searches for the right words of condolence*.

6   A friend *offers hollow words of congratulations* to someone who is *describing exactly* what she will do with the prize money.

7   Two people are *trying very hard to find the words* to admit that they love each other.

8   A ten-year-old child is *refusing to say 'thank you'* for a gift she has been given by an aunt who is *an expert at making people feel small.*

9   After many attempts, a man *finally arrives at* the description of his last night's dream.

10   A psychiatrist is asking a woman *very precise questions* about her fear of flying. The woman is *holding her real feelings back.*

BEWARE OF WORDS

Writers should always be wary of the ways in which words and phrases can use us, when we imagine we are using them. This is not to say that cliché, quotation, reference to, parody of, etc., are not useful tools – as long as we are aware that we are using them. In the struggle to develop our own individual voices, the following two quotations (which struck me as very original when I came across them) may be useful:

> 'The trouble with words is that you don't know whose mouths they've been in.'
>
> (Dennis Potter, talking about 'Patriotism')

> 'I can say I love London. I can say I love England. I can't say I love my country, because I don't know what that means.'
>
> (Alan Bennett)

8 Second draft

You now have your story, your characters and a first draft of your play. You have also begun to realise the themes you are working with, and you have gained confidence in the use of your own individual or collective voices as dramatic poets and storytellers. This is the moment when you will go right back to the start and see what is useful, what is redundant and what needs to be developed and added. We will start this chapter by revisiting some of the things we looked at earlier, in order to help us step back and take a look at the big picture.

All of the exercises in this chapter may be used in the following ways:

- By the individual playwright.
- As ongoing group workshop exercises.
- For further developing group-written performance pieces.

THE BIG PICTURE

Now we will go back to other aspects of composition, structure, etc., some of which we have touched on before. It is worth reminding ourselves of these, because now is the moment to look at the big picture of how your play will be put together. The following will equip you to move on to your second draft.

Exercise 106 Back-story

Remember the image of the suitcase? When your characters are intro-duced, they are all carrying the invisible suitcase packed with everything about their lives and the world they inhabit. Check through the luggage. Are there any items in the suitcase you need to throw out or replace?

Exercise 107 Opening scene

Your opening scene is key. We have already done quite a lot of work around the functions of the opening scene of a play. The phrase 'setting the agenda' has been used. The musical term 'overture' also comes to mind. A dictionary definition of the word: 'a piece of instrumental music intended as the introduction to an opera, oratorio, etc.'. 'Introduction' is the key word. The composer Gluck (eighteenth century) said that the function of the overture was 'to prepare the audience for the plot of the play'. An opening scene has a range of functions. Does yours include any or all of the following?

1   A sense of the 'world of the play' – contemporary, historical, mythical – that is specific to itself and therefore universal. The conventions, habits and nature of that world and how it operates.

2   Exposition: story. An introduction to the 'story-action' that prepares the audience. The facts (or supposed facts) the audience will be told.

3   Exposition: character. An introduction to the protagonist(s), either through themselves or on a reported basis. What they say about themselves, what others say about them.

4   Theme(s). Major topics that the play deals with, not necessarily spelled out but woven into the dialogue and the action.

5   Mood and atmosphere. The words that are used, their musicality, the rhythms of the dialogue.

Exercise 108 Exposition

Throughout the play you will be unpacking items from the suitcase that are useful to the telling of the story. Their functions include (a) allowing the audience to inhabit the world of the play, (b) allowing the audience to follow the journeys of the characters, (c) fuelling the action and (d) laying unexploded bombs.

Go through your play and ask the following questions:

1   Where and how do moments of exposition occur in your play?

2   Are there moments of exposition that serve no function, or hinder the development of the story?

3   What important bits of information, needed by the audience, are missing?

Exercise 109 The protagonist
Part one

The protagonist is the person (or persons) whose story the play is telling. The audience will be focussed on their journey. In some plays it is clear who that is (Hamlet; Vladimir and Estragon); in others, where there are a range of characters who have equal 'air time', it might not seem so obvious. You need to know, so ask yourself the following:

1 Whose story are you telling?

2 Has the focus begun to shift from your original protagonist towards another character?

3 How would it affect the story if you shifted the central focus to another character?

Part two – the protagonist

If you are unsure whose story is at the heart of the play, try writing it out (in story form) from the points of view of several of the characters.

Example 109.1

Retell Little Red Riding Hood from the point of view of: the grandmother; the mother; the wolf; the wood-cutter.

Exercise 110 The protagonist's goal/objective

There are two most important items in the protagonist's back-story: (a) their conscious needs, wants and desires (their *active* goal or objective), and (b) their unconscious needs, wants and desires (their *dormant* goal or objective). The motor of the play is when the two are in conflict. The outcome of the play will be the resolution of that conflict. Ask yourself the following questions:

1 What are your protagonist's active and dormant goals/objectives?

2 How much of a potential threat is the dormant goal to the active goal?

Exercise 111 The First Major Turning Point

The First Major Turning Point is where the protagonist's dormant goal/objective makes itself known. The active goal is challenged and the status quo is threatened or changed. This is now the driving force behind the play, and the main action begins here. From this moment, expectations are raised in the audience as to the outcome of the play. Ask yourself the following questions:

1 Where and how does the First Major Turning Point occur in your play?

2 Does it happen in a manner that is believable and appropriate to that world?

Exercise 112 The major conflicts of the story

The major conflicts in the story are given expression through the journey of the protagonist. These may operate on any or all of the following levels: the inner world (head, heart and soul), the immediate outer world (family, lovers, etc.), the wider social world (teachers, colleagues, etc.), the institutional world (police, professions, etc.), the historical or geographical circumstances of the world. Ask yourself the following questions:

1 What levels of conflict are depicted in your play?

2 Where and how are these expressed in the action?

Exercise 113 The protagonist under pressure

The *choices* the protagonist makes under pressure reveal deep character. The pressure is the developing conflict between the conscious and the unconscious. The greater the pressure, the deeper is the revelation of character. The events that flow from the increasing pressure on the protagonist provide the spine of the story. These events can be depicted as obstacles, reversals of fortune, strokes of luck, loss of nerve, a bold move, being thrown off-course, etc. Ask yourself the following questions:

1 Where do such events occur in your play?

2 Which are the major moments of pressure in which deep character is revealed?

3 Which are the incidental moments of pressure?

Exercise 114 Events as change

Each event is a moment of change: of mind, heart, conscience, circumstance, fortune, etc. The greater the crisis around the event, the greater the *value* (moral or material) of the change. As a general principle, as the story unfolds the stakes get higher. Ask yourself the following questions:

1 What is the progression of events?

2 If 1 is low pressure and 10 is high pressure, where would you place each event on the scale of 1–10?

3 As the story unfolds, the stakes get higher. Does the progression of events in your play reflect the increasing value of the changes taking place?

Exercise 115 The final outcome

From the First Major Turning Point, expectations have been raised in the audience as to the outcome. As the events evolve those expectations develop. The final outcome of the play is the biggest change of all. Everything has been put in place to support it. However surprising, shocking, delightful or unexpected it is, it must be appropriately believable to the events leading up to it. Ask yourself the following questions:

1 Does your protagonist achieve what she *thinks* she wants, or what she *really* needs, or what she *doesn't* desire?

2 Does she achieve it in a manner that is satisfying and appropriate to the journey the audience has been following?

Exercise 116 All the other characters

The journeys of all the other characters, however minor, should have the same patterns as that of the protagonist. Ask yourself the following questions:

1 What are the back-stories of your other characters?

2 What are the goals/objectives of all the other characters?

3 How are your other characters depicted through exposition, conflict, etc.?

4 What is the outcome for all the other characters?

Outcome

By addressing the questions above, you will have begun to consider where and how your first draft needs to be restructured, tightened and clarified. We have also seen that *change* is constantly happening, as the conflict between the conscious and unconscious of the protagonist develops.

DISSECTING THE TEXT

When writing a first draft we very often work on our instincts. In finding the story and setting the characters in motion you will not have bothered too much about the details of structure. You may have used some of the methods outlined in Chapter 5 (the postcard/index card exercise for example) to help with the overall shape, but not to the extent that these interrupt the flow of your imagination. Now is the time to see if the structure of the play holds true.

In my experience, the worst sort of conversation about where to take the play in the second draft is the speculative one, with lots of 'what if . . .' or 'I don't like . . .' etc. We need to be able to see *what is there* before we proceed to *what should be there*.

The following exercises enable us to dissect a play in a scientific manner: to take the machinery apart in order to reassemble it. The method can be used as a tool for developing a text at all draft stages. It is also a method for the director and actors to get to grips with a completed text in rehearsals. In both cases, the process is exactly the same.

Exercise 117 The text into units
Part one

1   Take the opening scene of a completed play and read it through.

2   You are going to dissect the scene. If you are working in a group, try not to get stuck on the choices you make. Attempt to arrive at some sort of consensus and move on.

3   Read the scene through again. This time, note where significant changes occur. By 'change' I mean a shift in action, in subject matter, in mood, etc. This can include directions as well as dialogue, and they may well occur in the middle of passages of both. In musical terms, we might say that the piece is shifting into a different key.

4   Each time one of these significant (key) changes occur, section off the text with a pencil line across the page. You are now breaking down the scene into its component units.

5   Read the united scene again. This time decide what the major action of each unit is. Use active verbs. Make that the title of the unit. Write the titles at the top of each unit. There is no right or wrong, just what you feel is the strongest, most dynamic (and often the simplest) expression of the main thing that occurs. Keep it to one simple sentence. When you read the example, see if you can come up with alternative section-titles of your own. (See Example 117.1.)

6   Write out the list of all the unit-titles. (See Example 117.2.)

7   On the basis of step 5, decide what the main action of the scene is. Title the scene. The unit-titles should all support the scene-title. Again, keep it to one simple sentence. (See Example 117.3.)

8   If change happens within a scene, what is the major change that happens in this scene? (See Example 117.4.)

9   What proposition or question does the scene put to us, in terms of how we are as human beings? This does not have to relate to the characters or the events. You can be quite abstract here. (See Example 117.5.)

Example 117.1

The dialogue between SKIPPER and OWNER in Chapter 7.

(Unit. The SKIPPER takes in the world.)
The SKIPPER, in a small pool of light. He has a small, battered tin globe, with all the time-zones, meridians, etc., on it. He spins it.

(Unit. The OWNER intrudes on the SKIPPER)

(Unit. The SKIPPER challenges the OWNER)
Skipper: (pointing to the small, battered globe) Put your finger down, anywhere. Bet your bottom dollar I've been there.
(He spins the globe)

(Unit. The OWNER pulls the SKIPPER up short)
(The OWNER puts his finger down)

(Unit. The SKIPPER sets the record straight)
Been there. Cancer, Capricorn, Equator, parallel. I've seen the lot.

(Unit. The OWNER lays down the law)
Owner: Safe home in harbour now.
Skipper: I'm not worn out yet. Nor me, nor boat.
Owner: She's pooped.
Skipper: My boat?
Owner: My boat.

Skipper: Yours by property, mine by feeling.
Owner: Time's up for that old tub.

(Unit. The OWNER softens the blow)
Skipper: No . . . never.
Owner: The firm recognises all you've done . . . (hands him a package)
            You'll have a tidy pension too.
(The SKIPPER takes out a watch on a chain from the package)

(Unit. The OWNER puts the boot in)
Owner: We're calling her in.
[Continue on your own]

Example 117.2

· The Skipper takes in the world.

· The Owner intrudes on the Skipper.

· The Skipper challenges the Owner.

· The Owner pulls the Skipper up short.

· The Skipper sets the record straight.

· The Owner softens the blow.

· The Owner puts the boot in.

[Continue on your own]

Example 117.3

Main action of the scene: the OWNER lays down the law.

Example 117.4

Main change (of circumstance or fortune) in the scene: the SKIPPER'S hopes are dashed.

Example 117.5

Our personal desires are controlled by impersonal forces.

Outcome

The word 'change' has come up a lot in the work we have been doing. In this exercise we have taken a whole scene apart to see where the major shifts of action, subject and mood are. The *unit-titles* all contained strong active verbs: intrude, challenge, soften the blow. These lay bare the inner-dynamic of the scene: a vigorous dynamic between two opposing views. And so the *scene-title* – the major action of the scene – contains and supports all the units of action within it.

I would use this method of dissecting the scene at the start of a rehearsal process with actors. It is much more effective than sitting around speculating about what is going on in the scene, what the character's 'motivations' are, etc. It is also equally useful in its application to a play in draft form.

Part two – sectioning the scene at draft-stage

1 Take a play that is in development (individual or group). Look at a scene or sequence from it, at first draft stage. Apply the above method to the scene or sequence, step by step. See how the process enables us to identify the changes that need to be made. In the examples I will be using a play by Manjinder Virk, with whom I recently worked as dramaturge. (See Examples 117.6 and 117.7.)

2 Take your own opening scene and apply the same method to it. Be as rigorous as you were with the extant play in the first part of the exercise. Where are the shifts and what are they? What is the inner-dynamic? Do the section-titles support the scene-title? Where is the flab? Where are the missing support-beams?

3 Repeat the above process for all the scenes of the play.

4 Write out the list of all the scene-titles for the whole play.

5 On the basis of step 3, decide what the main action title of the whole play is and write it out. (See Example 117.8.)

6 On the basis of the whole exercise, where are the gaps? What passages, sections or scenes are redundant? What aspects of exposition are missing? Which characters need to be fleshed out or written out?

Example 117.6

Sequence from draft one of *Glow*, by Manjinder Virk.

KULWINDER is a young Asian girl of 14. ANTONY, her best friend, is a young white boy of 13. The sequence takes place about one-third of the way into the play. In the play, KUL is intent on winning a boxing competition she has been training for. 'Proving herself' is very much on her mind. In the sequence, she is challenged by the news that ANT brings.

(Section. ANT seeks to establish if KUL shares the same information.)

[ANTONY enters]

Ant: Did you see her? Did you Kul?

Kul: What you on about?

Ant: Tracey Ramsey!

(Section. KUL derides the subject in hand.)
Kul: That slag.

(Section. KUL show some interest in the subject.)
What about her?

(Section. ANT pursues his main enquiry)
Ant: Did you see her?

Kul: Ain't seen her since before the summer holidays.

(Section. KUL cross-examines ANT)
Why? She preggers?

(Section. ANT gives a full account of the facts.)
Ant: No, she was on telly!

Kul: Crimewatch?

Ant: No, Popstars, I saw her with my own eyes!

Kul: What?

Ant: She was auditioning for Popstars! She was actually on TV Kul, Tracey Ramsey, they showed her face for ages and she sang 'Can't Get You Out of My Head'.

Kul: No!

Ant: She looked really good, not like Kylie but she can sing an' that.

Section titles:

- ANT seeks to establish if KUL shares the same information.
- KUL derides the subject in hand.
- KUL shows some interest in the subject.
- ANT pursues his main enquiry.
- KUL cross-examines ANT.
- ANT gives a full account of the facts.

Possible sequence titles:

- ANT unsettles KUL.

- KUL and ANT spar.

- ANT fails to impress KUL.

Development points for the script:

Manjinder and I discussed the function of the sequence as an important moment that reveals much about KUL's insecurities. By taking it apart, we decided the threat posed by Tracey Ramsey's TV success needed to be more immediate. We made the following decisions:

- Instead of the subject matter of Tracey Ramsey on the TV being reported by ANT, make it more immediate by bringing it into the onstage action.

- Make Tracey Ramsey more of a threat to KUL. Allow KUL to be more rattled by the idea of Tracey Ramsey on the TV.

- Both of the above will give more fuel to KUL's fighting mood.

Example 117.7

Sequence from draft two of *Glow*, by Manjinder Virk: In the light of the development points, the head of the rewritten sequence was strengthened as follows.

(Section. ANT winds KUL up.)
[ANTONY and KULWINDER are watching the TV together.]

Ant: Oh my god, it's Tracey Ramsey.

Kul: What?

Ant: Oh my god, it's Tracey Ramsey!

Kul: No.

Ant: Oh my god! It's Tracey Ramsey!

(Section. KUL slaps ANT down.)

Kul: Alright! I heard you the first time.

Ant: She's on telly, Kul!

Kul: I can see that.

(Section. KUL degrades the subject matter.)
What is she wearing? She looks a right slapper.

(Section. ANT rubs KULs nose in the dirt.)

Ant: I can't believe they're showing her for ages, look at her, I can't believe we go to school with her and she's on telly! Look at her!

Kul: Alright, don't give yourself a heart attack.

Ant: I hope she gets through.

Kul: No chance.

Ant: I can't believe it.

Kul: Will you calm down, you're doing my head in!

Ant: She looked really good, don't you think? Not like Christina Aguilera but she can sing an' that.

Example 117.8

I have already quoted what might be the main action title for *Hamlet*: 'by failing to take revenge on his father's murder, a young prince brings death and destruction to the whole court'. This contains the dilemma the protagonist is presented with, and the outcome of his failure to deal with it. I say 'might be', because you could well identify things differently. The point is that, if either of us were to produce the play, we would need to have a clear idea of what the main thrust of the action is. Similarly, when we are writing a play, we need to be able to identify the major arc of the story.

Outcome

We have seen how a sequence, a scene, an act, a whole play can be taken apart in a scientific manner, in order to identify (a) what is happening, (b) where the gaps are, and (c) what is redundant. We have also seen how the 'action titles' reveal the inner dynamic that leads to the major action of the whole play.

CONSTANT CHANGE

We have looked at change happening with the major events, beginning with the First Major Turning Point. However, change is happening constantly, to greater or lesser degrees. We saw how an opening scene can be broken down into sections, each of which shift to a new active drive. We saw how these changes all lead to, and support, the main change in the scene.

In the following exercises we will look at how 'change' happens on a moment-to-moment basis. Again, these are exercises that actors and directors often use at the start of rehearsals, to get to grips with the dynamics of the story. They are equally useful to the writer, in terms of fine-tuning the script as it develops.

Exercise 118 Attack, retreat, stand ground
Part one

All psychological interactions between people can be categorised under any one of three active headings: I attack, I retreat, I stand my ground.

Examples 118.1

I criticise you (I attack). I apologise to you (I retreat). I justify my behaviour (I stand my ground). 'Criticise', 'apologise' and 'justify' are verbs for psychological actions. We can also describe psychological actions with verbs for physical actions. I 'bulldoze' you (I attack). I 'cave in' (I retreat). I 'dig my heels in' (I stand my ground).

Part two – attack, retreat, stand ground

Under the three headings, write lists of actives (single words or well-known expressions) that can be applied to psychological interactions. High-level actions appear at the top of the list, moving down to low-level actions at the bottom.

Examples 118.2

I attack	I retreat	I stand my ground
Annihilate	Shrink from	Refuse to budge
Berate	Withdraw	Defy
Command	Concede	Resist
Degrade	Surrender	Hold fast
Educate	Throw in the towel	Sit tight
Humour	Back down	Ignore
Prod	Collapse	Deny
Tickle	Abandon	Dig in
Etc.	Etc.	Etc.

Exercise 119 Actioning the text
Part one

Take a passage from a play that you have united. Bearing in mind the title of the units of action , decide upon the 'active' of each unit of speech (or 'beat' as it may be termed).

Example 119.1

(Unit. The OWNER lays down the law)

Owner: [I place you] Safe home in harbour now.

Skipper: [I refuse the offer] I'm not worn out yet. [I make my stand] Nor me, nor boat.

Owner: [I judge] She's pooped.

Skipper: [I contest] My boat?

Owner: [I specify] My boat.

Skipper: [I claim] Yours by property, mine by feeling.

Owner: [I condemn] Time's up for that old tub.

Part two – actioning the text

Take a passage from your own play that you have sectioned. Bearing in mind the title of the section, decide upon the 'active' of each unit of speech (or beat). Does each beat lock into and support the action title of the section? Where is the flab? What is missing?

Outcome

We have now seen that 'change' is constantly happening in a play as inexorably as the second-hand ticks away on the clock. There may be passages in a play where 'idle conversation' is being depicted, but there is nothing idle in the construction of those passages. Everything is there for a purpose: to move the story along, to prepare for the next major change. Everything in the play is preparing for the final outcome.

THE FOUNDATIONS OF THE PLAY

We have seen how a play is 'about' a subject matter (the major arc of the story) and 'about' a theme (a universal human concern). These are linked by something that lies at the heart of every story: some major question or proposition about human life and activity. It is never spelled out for the audience, but the writer must be clear what that is, for it is the foundation of the play and the reason for writing it. It can be expressed in a clear, one-sentence statement. The outcome of the story and its theme will answer or prove/disprove the major questions or propositions.

A major question that the story of Macbeth asks might be: 'If we reject our better instincts in order to pursue our desire for earthly power, do we forfeit our right to spiritual salvation?'

A major proposition that the story of Little Red Riding Hood presents might be: 'We can fully develop only if we reject the rules and put ourselves to the test.'

Never spelled out for the audience, but constantly suggesting itself through the story and its themes, this statement prompts questions and expectations in the minds of the audience. This is what hooks us into the story and keeps us there until the final outcome.

The major-question posed by the play Macbeth might be: 'Will Macbeth manage to redeem himself?'

The major proposition placed by Little Red Riding Hood might be: 'Will Little Red get through the test she has set herself?'

When you are writing your first draft, concentrating on getting the story out and developing the characters, you should not worry too much about major questions and propositions. There may be writers who start from a question or an abstract proposition, but I wouldn't advise it. What gets us going as writers is the excitement of the story, the creation of new worlds, the god-like manipulation of characters. Now that you are onto your second draft, it is time to give some thought to what may lie at the root of your play, what it is really 'about'.

Exercise 120 The essence of the play
Participants: All groups, individual

The major proposition or question is the essence of your play: the big idea or abstract thought you have (probably unconsciously) been dealing with. Having followed through all the exercises in this chapter so far, what do you think is the big, major question or proposition your play is addressing. One method of discovering what this might be is as follows.

You will have already done some of this work.

1 Section the scenes and title them: (a) major action, (b) major change, (c) major proposition or question.

2   If the play is structured on acts, title these also: (a) major action, (b) major change, (c) major proposition or question.

3   List all the major propositions or questions posed by the scenes.

4   List all the major propositions or questions posed by the acts. (See Examples 120.1.)

5   What does step 4 suggest, in terms of a general preoccupation with certain thoughts, ideas or questions? Is there a pattern? Do some thoughts arise in different forms? Are there words that resonate with each other? Are there dominant ideas? What images arise? (See Examples 120.2.)

6   On the basis of step 5, write out a few possible propositions or questions for the whole play. Try for a simple two-part sentence, in which the essence of the play is captured. (See Examples 120.3.)

7   Choose one of the above.

8   Test it out on the play. Do all the parts of the play, in some way, cast light on it, resonate with it, or reflect it?

9   When you have landed on the proposition or question that seems to embody the essence of what the play is rooted in, write it down on a card.

10 Stick the card on the top of your desk or writing-machine.

11 Re-write your play with this directly in front of you.

12 Remember: you can always change it if the play goes in new directions.

Examples 120.1

Major questions for the five acts of a play:

- Act One: Do we swim together or do we sink together?
- Act Two: How do we create new life from death?
- Act Three: How do we feel about going against the flow?
- Act Four: How do we calm down and see that we can survive?
- Act Five: Why don't those in power listen to children?

Examples 120.2

- Words that resonate: swim, sink, flow.
- Words that resonate: sink, death, powerful.

- Words that resonate: together, create, life, feel, calm, survive, listen, children.
- Images: swim together, sink together, going against the flow, listen to children.

Examples 120.3

- If we create a world in which we fear each other, what is the future for our children?
- When we accept what we are told without question, we cannot complain if we are not listened to.
- Do we allow the negative forces in the world to dominate our lives, or do we swim against the tide?
- Do we look for the litter in life, or do we look for the swans?

Outcome

- We have seen how, by dissecting a whole scene, the internal dynamic can be exposed. By giving active titles to the sections and the scene, we discovered what the major action of the scene is, and what the major change in the scene is. By applying that method to the whole play, we have seen how the full arc of the story is supported by all the other structural elements.
- We have seen how the major theme or themes of the play are suggested from the outset, through deliberate placing and weighting of key words and images.
- We have seen how the major theme, woven into the main story action, gives rise to the major proposition/question upon which the play is based. As the foundation of the play, it is reflected in and resonates with every moment of the play.

The *major proposition/question* is the foundation of the play.

A *beat* (unit of speech) is the smallest dramatic moment.

A *section* (unit of dialogue, or episode) is a sequence of related beats.

A *scene* is a sequence of sections, introducing and completing a significant event.

An *act* is a sequence of scenes, dramatically concluding a series of significant events.

An *event* is a major pressure moment and turning point for the protagonist.

The *first major turning point* is the event that kick-starts the plot.

The *plot* is charted by the events.

The *story* develops around the plot.

The *themes* are woven into the story.

The *final outcome* concludes the major theme of the story.

The *major theme* is expressed in the major proposition behind the story.

The *major proposition/question* is the foundation of the play.

Before you proceed with your second draft, there are a few more items we should consider.

BECAUSE OR IF

Let us imagine that there are only two types of play. One has a major proposition at its heart that uses the word 'because'; the other uses the word 'if'.

Exercise 121 Because

Complete the following sentences (do not include the word 'if'):

- People kill because . . .
- People love because . . .
- People make art because . . .
- People go to war because . . .
- People have prejudices because . . .
- People work because . . .

Examples 121.1

- People kill because they are full of anger.
- People love because it makes them feel good.
- People make art because they have imaginations.
- People go to war because they think they are right.
- People have prejudices because it makes them feel superior.
- People work because they need money.

Exercise 122 If

Complete the following sentences (do not include the word 'because'):

- If people kill . . .
- If people love . . .
- If people make art . . .
- If people go to war . . .
- If people have prejudices . . .
- If people work . . .

Examples 122.1

- If people kill they destroy themselves.
- If people love they must give it freely.
- If people make art they can change the world.
- If people go to war they should be sure it is right.
- If people have prejudices they can be easily led.
- If people work they can earn the money they need to live on.

Exercise 123 People kill because . . .

Complete the sentence five times, starting with your original one.

Examples 123.1

- People kill because they are full of anger.
- People kill because they see it on the television.
- People kill because they are afraid.
- People kill because they don't value human life.
- People kill because they think it will solve the problem.

Exercise 124 If people kill . . .

Complete the sentence five times, starting with your original one.

Examples 124.1

- If people kill they destroy themselves.
- If people kill they must be prepared to face the consequences.
- If people kill they have failed themselves.
- If people kill they can never be happy again.
- If people kill they must be given the chance to redeem themselves.

Outcome

In the previous exercises we have explored what the choice of writing an 'if play' or a 'because play' implies.

- 'Because' tends to seek a closed answer – and therefore a solution: people will stop killing if their anger is removed. It also accepts as a given that killing is, under present conditions, a factor of human life.
- 'If' tends not to seek a root cause. It accepts that killing might go on, but is more concerned with exploring the consequences of the action: how exactly does the act of killing destroy the individual killer?
- 'Because' plays tend to offer a solution to a social issue. The plays of Bernard Shaw and Bertolt Brecht seek to expose the mechanisms of a corrupt or unjust society, and in doing so propose a better system of living. Agitprop theatre, Forum theatre and some forms of Theatre-in-Education seek to diagnose the root causes of social or political ills, and suggest to the audience ways in which they can be overcome.
- 'If' plays tend not to question the underlying structures of society. They tend to look at how individual human beings operate within the scope of their circumstances. In his play *Private Lives*, Noel Coward is not concerned with questioning the society that has produced his spoiled, rich protagonists; he is looking at the consequences of infatuation.
- Perhaps the most interesting plays contain both the 'because' and the 'if'. Chekhov tends towards the 'if' – he certainly doesn't propose that Masha would cease to be unhappy should the wealth of the world be equally divided. But the social levels in the plays – masters and servants, petty bureaucrats and landowners – draw a picture of a society that corrupts people's relations. In her plays, Caryl Churchill makes it clear that unjust social relations bear down on the lives of the women she depicts. In her play *A Raisin in the Sun*, Lorraine Hansberry asks what happens when a black man dreams of achieving a better existence, and exposes the roots of a society that seeks to deny him that dream.

- At all stages of our writing, we can now ask ourselves: how much 'because' and how much 'if'?

SUBPLOT

Secondary sequences of actions are often termed the subplot. The characters involved are of lesser importance, but their function is no less vital for that. The subplot may be closely linked to the main story, running parallel to it or as a contrast to it. In Elizabethan and Jacobean drama the subplots mirrored the main plot, often as low comedy and with characters of lower social status. In Shakespeare's *As You Like It*, the developing love story of the aristocratic Rosalind and Orlando is paralleled by the courtships, wooings and fallings out of shepherdesses and foresters. The function of the subplots there is to cast different lights on the main themes of the play. In *Macbeth*, the subplot of the loving and honourable Macduff family serves to contrast with the hate-filled and treacherous Macbeths. In both cases, they illuminate the main themes of the play.

Exercise 125 Secondary characters

Ask yourself the following questions:

1   Does your play contain secondary characters and sequences of actions?

2   What is the dramatic function of the secondary characters?

3   Do the journeys of the secondary characters lock into the main plot and the themes of the play?

4   If your play does not contain subplot, would it benefit from doing so?

CHARACTER: OBJECTIVES

Earlier in this chapter, we looked at how the characters are always 'doing' (the actives behind the dialogue). From moment to moment, section to section, scene to scene, etc., they have goals and objectives they wish to achieve (consciously or unconsciously). This applies to all the characters, but most particularly to the protagonist(s).

Exercise 126 The protagonist's objectives

Ask yourself the following questions about your protagonist:

1 What is her objective in the play?
2 What is her objective in the scene?
3 What is her objective in the sequence?
4 What is her objective in the moment?
5 What is her objective in life?

Examples 126.1

· Macbeth's objective in the play is *to survive.*

· Macbeth's objective in life is *to satisfy his ambitions and remain a good human being.*

Examples 126.2

· Little Red Riding Hood's objective in the story is *to deliver the food to grandmother.*

· When Little Red promises to go straight to grandma's, her objective is *to be an obedient daughter.*

· When she picks the flowers, Little Red's objective is *to please herself.*

· When she sees the wolf dressed up as grandma, Little Red's objective is *to get reassurance.*

· Little Red's objective in life might be *to discover all that life has to offer.*

SCENE-SHAPES

We have looked at 'change' and how that is happening all the time in a narrative. Major changes occur within scenes: the fortunes of the protagonists have changed by the end of the scene. They may be large or small changes, emotional or material changes, etc., depending on the story you are writing and the needs of the narrative; but the characters leave the scene changed in some way.

I have already mentioned how actors can speak of dealing with an audience in terms of doing battle. It is useful to use the battleground image when thinking of a scene in a play: someone will be the victor, someone will be defeated (or they may be stalemate after a struggle). The following exercises will use the shapes of the square and the triangle as the literal sites of struggle.

For the purposes of the exercises, I would like us to think of a scene as a sequence of actions that take place within a continuous time frame.

- Think of a scene as having the shape of a square. Think of it as an emotional battlefield, or football pitch.
- The scene contains two characters, A and B. We know nothing about them at the start. We come to the scene allowing them equal status (space on the pitch).
- By the end of the scene, character B has 'invaded' the pitch to the extent that character A is pushed into a corner.
- By the end of the next scene, character A has regained a lot of ground.
- By the end of the next scene, character B has been joined by character C. They have nearly driven character A off the pitch.

Exercise 127 Pushing the boundaries

1   You have three characters: A, B and C.

2   Place A and B in a situation. Keep it simple. Scene one is the square.

3   Write notes on the first three scenes of a play. They will begin and end according to the progression of shapes suggested below.

4   Bear in mind that, even though the final scene ends with B and C 'cornering' A, this does not mean they will (as the play progresses) *finally* win the battle.

Start of scene one: A and B are sharing a social moment. They seem to have equal share of the pitch.

End of scene one: B has pushed A onto the defensive.

Start of scene two: A is still on the defensive. Something occurs that gives an opening.

End of scene two: A has regained much ground and B is on the defensive.

Start of scene three: A is now confident that he has nearly gained control of the whole pitch. C now enters the pitch and teams up with B. Together they push A into a very tight corner.

Example 127.1

Scene One

- Charles and Sita work in the same office.
- They are standing by the water dispenser in the corridor, talking.

- Someone has been sending abusive e-mails to other members of staff.
- By the end of the scene, Sita has implied that Charles has been the one responsible.

Scene Two

- Later, Charles overhears Sita on the phone. She is repeating to someone else what she has said to Charles earlier.
- By the end of the scene, Charles has confronted Sita. He says that she is making her accusations because they have both applied for promotion to the same post. He accuses her of attempting to ruin his reputation within the company.
- Sita, rather unconvincingly, tries to defend herself, saying that she did not know they were rivals for the post.

Scene Three

- After lunch, Charles is on the phone to the boss. He is asking if he can come and talk to him. He has a complaint to make about the conduct of another member of staff.
- Sita is working on her computer, but is clearly agitated by what she overhears.
- Jean enters, with a hard copy of an e-mail which she claims to have downloaded from Charles' address.
- Sita looks at her own mail and discovers a similar message.
- Supported by Jean, Sita remounts her attack on Charles, who seems to have no explanation as to how these messages have been sent via his machine.

Exercise 128 Manipulating the triangle

This is another method of exploring scene-shape and the dynamics that take place within a scene, leading to change by the end of the scene.

1 You are going to write a short (three-step) outline for a narrative that features three characters.

2 At step one, we know nothing about the characters. As far as we know, they have equal status.

3 In the course of the scene there will be shifts in alliances, status, etc. Remember all the work on 'actioning' and find strong actions to title the sequences.

4 To depict the shifting nature of what is going on between the characters, we will use the image of a triangle.

5 A close alliance between characters is represented by the closeness of the points of the triangle. Draw the changing shape of the triangle as alliances shift.

Example 128.1

• *Start of scene*: Tanya, Stuart and Barb *conspire* to arrange a surprise eightieth birthday party for their mother.

• *Middle of scene*: Stuart and Barb *doubt* Tanya's commitment to the project.

• *End of scene*: Tanya and Stuart and Barb *abandon* the whole idea.

Exercise 129 The bridge over troubled waters

We have explored scene-shapes as square battlefields and manipulated triangles. We have seen how we can leave a scene with a change of values (material, emotional, situational, spiritual, etc.). It can also be useful to think of the structure of a scene as a bridge that takes us from *opening moment A (dry land)* to *closing moment Z (dry land)*. The steps the characters take across the bridge represent what the characters do. The water under the bridge represents their unconscious.

1 Take the last example given above (the Tanya, Stuart and Barb story). The middle sequence of the scene is titled 'Stuart and Barb doubt Tanya's commitment to the project'.

2 Make the middle sequence more complex by adding two more actives. (See Example 129.1.)

3 The characters are at the middle of the bridge, where the water is deepest. We know from the 'actions' what the characters are doing. Think about what is going on under the surface.

4 Write the middle sequence. We know that the scene starts with them in harmony, and that it ends in disharmony. Explore fully this middle sequence. How do the characters move forward, so that they can reach the other side of the bridge?

Example 129.1

• Stuart and Barb *doubt* Tanya's commitment to the project.

• Tanya and Stuart *accuse* Barb of manipulating them.

• Barb and Tanya *line up against* Stuart.

Outcome

By visualising scenes as squares, triangles and bridges we have explored further how they have formal underlying structures. The structure of the scenes will finally support the structure of the whole play. As we will now see, the shape of the whole story can be visualised just as formally.

STORY-SHAPES

In Chapter 1, we saw how a story could be circular, ending where it begins: Exercise 27. We now look at the range of other formal structures that are available for you to use.

1   The linear story. Continuous chronology. At its most classical it observes the dramatic unities of time, place and action.
2   The 'Chinese box' story. One large story containing stories within stories.
3   A sequence of separate stories. Not linked by characters or dramatic narrative. Possibly related to each other by theme, location, etc.
4   One long story interrupted by other stories.
5   The relay race story. A sequence of stories connected by characters.
6   Parallel stories. Two or more stories, unconnected in narrative. Possibly differing in time, place, etc. Possibly related to each other by theme, etc.
7   The flashback story. One long story, with the time-sequence thrown.
8   The circular story, ending up where it started.

GENRE

Genre.
Dictionary definition: kind, category, or sort, especially of literary or artistic work.

Generic.
Dictionary definition: applicable or referring to a whole class or group.

Polonius:	The actors are come hither, my lord.
Hamlet:	Buzz, buzz.
Polonius:	Upon mine honour –

Hamlet: Then come each actor on his ass –
Polonius: The best actors in the world, either for tragedy, comedy,
             history, pastoral, pastoral-comical, historical-pastoral, trag-
             ical-historical, tragical-comical-historical-pastoral; scene
             indivisible, or poem unlimited.

(Hamlet. Act 2, Scene 2)

It is interesting that Polonius, once he has listed the two major (Western) dramatic categories – tragedy and comedy – then goes on to complexify them. It is as if Shakespeare is acknowledging that the notion of a 'genre' is not quite as fixed as it might seem to be in the dictionary sense. The tragic can be the comical. The tragical-comical can be the pastoral.

So how do we define the genre of play we are writing? Do we need to know what category of play we are writing? I would suggest that it is a useful exercise, in that it might help us locate the *territories* we are working in. By territories I mean *dramatic style* and *form*.

A composer will know which form (classical or modern) they are working in: sonata, symphony, rap, reggae, blues, etc. Even if they are creating something that is none of these, something that seems entirely new, they will be in some way drawing on or responding to these or other traditional forms. We have seen how *Waiting for Godot* exhibits the remnants of classical structure; and how *Attempts on her Life* exhibits the remnants of *Waiting for Godot*. As playwrights, we are working within a tradition that goes back to the plays of Classical Greece, which in their turn take us back to the epic tales that came out of the Mediterranean basin, the Middle East, India and beyond. The play you are writing may not seem to fit into any particular category, but it will be drawing on one or another, or a few of them. What are they? Polonius begins with 'tragedy' and 'comedy', so let us start there.

There are (in the Western cultural tradition, which is the one I am positioned in) two great views of human life, which have come down to us from the Greek and Roman playwrights:

- The tragic: an unhappy ending to lives in struggle. Life is meaningless, full of unrelieved pain, with no redemption and doomed to failure and despair. Or, *the story of the loss of human values*.
- The comic: a happy ending to lives in struggle. Life as meaningful, compensatory, redemptive and full of hope. Or, *the story of the gain of human values*.

Where is your play positioned in relationship to the two views? Most likely it will seem to float somewhere between the two. This is fine, since the words 'tragic' and 'comic' are rather debased in the world we live in. How do we write a tragedy when any news story uses the word to encapsulate any sorry event? An Iraqi child maimed by a bomb (terrible, but not tragic), the closing down of a pet sanctuary (sad, but not tragic). How do we write comedy when every TV programme encourages us to giggle at anything and think about nothing? A wife meets her husband's mistress on a reality-show and slaps her face (hilarious but not comic), a stand-up comedian spews out gags about TV shows and 'relationships' (worth a snigger, but not comic).

If the categories of 'pure' comedy and tragedy have become diluted into a range of sub-genres, it is helpful to identify what those might be.

Tragedy: types of narrative forms in which the outcome tends to be the downfall of the protagonist, or a negative view of the human condition.

- Domestic tragedy.
- Melodrama.
- Murder mystery.
- Thriller.
- High opera.
- Psychological drama.
- Social drama.
- Ghost story.
- Family saga.

Comedy: types of narrative forms in which the outcome tends to be the redemption of the protagonist, or a positive view of the human condition.

- Domestic comedy.
- Comedy of manners.
- Romantic comedy.
- Light comedy.
- Satire.
- Situation comedy.
- Farce.
- Pantomime.
- Operetta.
- Music hall.
- Musical comedy.
- Sketch.

Drama today tends away from the two 'pure' categories. For our own work, it is useful to see how any new story can borrow from either of them, and from their sub-categories. Before asking yourself what genre/genres your own play is drawing on, it is worth taking another narrative and reworking it in various forms.

Exercise 130 Re-telling the tale

1   Take a well-known story/tale/myth (not a play) that is known to the whole group.

2   The simpler the story the better. Go for something that does not appear to have a great deal of depth or complexity: a folk-tale, fairy story, fable, etc. As we have been using *Little Red Riding Hood* already, I am going to stay with her in this exercise.

3   Get the facts of the story clear. Write out the story, or re-tell it round the circle. Go back and add in any details that seem necessary. In both cases, keep the narrative quite simple.

4   Write out a list of Little Red's significant actions in the story. Keep strictly to *events* as opposed to *thoughts* and *feelings*. (See Example 130.1.)

5   Rewrite or re-tell the story in a number of different ways:

   •   As a rap song.
   •   As a shock-horror TV news report.
   •   As a speech at a feminist conference.
   •   As a piece of gossip. [See Examples 130.2(a)–130.2(d).]

6   Rewrite the story in a number of different dramatic genres or forms. You can use the whole story, or certain sections of it. You can use dialogue, narration, stage-directions, etc.

   •   As a Greek tragedy, in which she is the doomed heroine.
   •   As a courtroom drama, in which she is on trial for attempted murder.
   •   As an urban teenage love-comedy, in which she is a streetwise kid. [See Examples 130.3(a)–130.3(c).]

7   Look at the play you are writing. In its style and form, does it lend itself to any particular category? Are there different categories of form and style in it? Have you deliberately drawn on different genres to create specific effects, moods, etc.? Did you think you were setting out to write in one genre, when in effect the material actually lends itself to another?

8   Look at any new play that is in development.

Example 130.1

- She hears that her Gran is ill.
- She puts on her red cape.
- She picks up the basket of food.
- She promises to take the path straight through the wood.
- She makes her way through the wood.
- She sees the flowers by the side of the path.
- She goes into the wood to pick the flowers.
- She gets lost in the wood.
- She meets the wolf.
- Etc.

Example 130.2(a)

She's a hood in a wood
An' that ain't so good
When her ma's gotta fright
Cos her gran's uptight
On account of the night
On the other side of the wood
Of the wood
Of the wood
So she takes the food
Cos the gal ain't rude
An' she struts her stuff
But it ain't enough
Etc.

Example 130.2(b)

Good evening, this is the 10 o'clock news. Disturbing reports are coming in of a young girl sent into the forest, alone, by her mother. She claims that she sent her daughter on an errand of mercy, to take food to her dying grandmother on the other side of the forest. But experts say that the wolves are out in force at this time of the year and the child's red coat will surely catch their blood-shot eyes, as she makes her way through this lonely and dangerous place . . . etc.

Example 130.2(c)

Women! We are told to stay inside at night! We are told that the world is a jungle and we must be protected from it! But I say we must take our example from Little Red. When her grandmother lay sick and ill on the other side of the forest, did she say 'I am too afraid to step outside?' No. She put on her brightest clothes and strode out into the night. And when she saw the flowers by the side of the path, did she say 'I must obey my mother in all things?' No, she saw those flowers, she desired those flowers, she would have those flowers . . . etc.

Example 130.2(d)

That mother should be ashamed of herself. Haven't you heard? The whole village is talking about it. Well . . . I'm not one to gossip, but you just have to look at them. No father, of course, that's the trouble. And the poor old grandmother, left all alone on the other side of the wood. Didn't you see the girl . . . in that ridiculous red coat with the hood . . . going off into the trees tonight? Mind you, she's no better than her mother, with all her airs and graces, etc.

Example 130.3(a)

[The GODS OF THE WOODS look down on LITTLE RED as she goes off the path to pick the flowers.]

Gods: Now see, how she spurns her mother,
        How she strays from the path of virtue.
        She is moving from the light into the dark,
        She is stepping towards her final destruction.
Red: Why should I always bow down to my mother?
        She behaves as if she were a queen, as if I am her slave.
        I will have those flowers, I will wear them in my hair,
        I will be far more beautiful than she ever was.
Gods: Then she is cursed,
        For when a child rebels against a parent,
        Then the world will fall apart.
        She will live to regret her actions.
        Etc.

Example 130.3(b)

[LITTLE RED is in the dock. She is being cross-examined by the prosecuting attorney.]

Attorney: So, Ms Hood, you say that, on the day of the attempted crime, your mother asked you to visit your grandmother?
Red: She was very ill and she lives on her own, on the other side of the wood.

Attorney: And you say that you are very fond of your grandmother?
Red: She made me this red coat.
Attorney: That does not answer the question, Ms Hood, please answer the question. If you love your grandmother so much, why, when the police entered the house, was she found in a pool of blood?
Red: You're confusing me! The wolf . . .
Attorney: Ha! The wolf!
Judge: I must ask you not to confuse the witness by constantly making fun of her . . . etc.

Example 130.3(c)

[RED meets WULF in the park. She wears a red sweatshirt and carries a plastic bag of groceries.]

Wulf: Hey, Red . . . where you been?
Red: You just keep your paws off me, Wulf.
Wulf: So how come you were sweet on me last week?
Red: I don't run with your pack no more.
Wulf: She's mummy's little girl now, eh? Come on, give me a break.
Red: Like a leg? I gotta go. I got responsibilities.
Wulf: To yourself Red! You got responsibilities to yourself.
 To us.
 Etc.

Outcome

By investigating the story and by identifying its major actions (steps 3 and 4 in the exercise), we discovered that beneath its simple surface, it offered the possibilities for a tale that can be retold in a range of ways. Each experiment with genre and form revealed layers to the story, all of which throw different lights upon it. All of them are valid as a means of telling the story.

In *Waiting for Godot*, Estragon and Vladimir at one point go into a music hall comedy routine with hats. The play ends with Estragon's trousers falling down. These things happen in a play where the protagonists are clearly on the edge of some sort of despair about their lives. Chekhov calls *The Seagull* 'a comedy', although everyone is clearly unhappy and one of the protagonists shoots himself at the end.

When we are building our story, it is well worth asking ourselves what genres we are playing with and why. When someone asks 'what type of play are you writing?' we may not be able to say 'it's a tragedy' or 'it's a comedy', but it does help if we have an idea ourselves of the genre-devices that we are using. Back to Polonius, perhaps?

STORY-TYPES

We have seen that we are always drawing on forms of the comic and the tragic, even if those two genres do not exist today in a pure sense. It is also useful to ask ourselves what 'type' of story we are telling. It has been said that there are only a very limited number of story-types, and that they can be found in all cultures. I am not sure if there is a definitive list of story-types, but here are some I have identified. Add your own suggestions to these. Ask yourself if your own play leans towards any of them.

- *The revenge story*. Jacobean plays, such as *The Revengers Tragedy*, come to mind, although revenge stories can also be comic: classic French farce can revolve around the cuckolded husband taking revenge for his humiliation.
- *The redemption story*. Those stories in which the protagonist redeems herself from a life of sin, or from past mistakes. Schiller's *Mary Stuart*, in which the Queen goes to the scaffold as a martyr to her faith, having risen above the follies of her life, is an example. Timberlake Wertenbaker's *Our Country's Good* is about the redeeming nature of creativity. Shakespeare's *As You Like It* can be seen as the depiction of the redeeming power of love. It is also a good example of a play in which the types of play are mixed: it begins as a potential revenge-tragedy and moves into the area of 'pastoral-comical'.
- *The rite-of-passage story*. Stories in which the protagonist faces a test or series of tests in order to grow and develop as a human being. Little Red Riding Hood and many folk-tales from around the world figure largely here.
- *The quest story*. Those stories in which the protagonist seeks the object or the answer that will solve a major life-problem. Oedipus is on a quest to solve a riddle, the answer to which will prove his downfall. The knights of King Arthur set out on a quest to find the Holy Grail. In Tennessee Williams' *Camino Real*, Kilroy is on a quest to discover how to leave the place he is trapped in.
- *The mistaken identity story*. In Shakespeare's *Twelfth Night*, the characters discover who they truly are through being seen as who they are not. Mistaken identity or transformation into other beings – often animals – feature in folk-tales and myths across the world (often in the form of rite-of-passage stories).

There are also categories of plays that are culturally specific in their form and content. Some of them are very local, and are a shorthand acknowledgement of a type of play that comes out of a certain geography or climate. Again, it may be useful to consider if your own play draws upon or resonates with any of these, or any other categories you might add to the ones I suggest here.

- *The Jamaican 'yard play'*. Stories that are set in the communal back-yard, where all social interactions take place – a sort of democratic space in which the lives of the characters are played out, and in which some European notions of 'privacy' do not. *Moon On A Rainbow Shawl*, by Errol John, is an example of such a play.
- *The 'prairie porch play'*. I came across this when working in Winnipeg, Canada. This is a type of play set (like the Jamaican 'yard play') in a climate that encourages people to spend a great deal of time sitting outside on the open veranda.
- *The 'kitchen sink play'*. This – slightly derogatory – term was attached to a type of play that emerged in the UK in the 1950s. They were plays by the generation that included Arnold Wesker, which depicted working class characters in their domestic surroundings: a revolt against the previous generations of middle-class plays set in drawing rooms.
- *The 'street-cred' play*. Plays that depict young, urban life in Western culture. Often fast-moving and with an edge of violence, borrowing from the rhythms of film and television.
- *Masque, pageant and ceremonial plays*. Formal works, often drawing upon specific cultural rituals.

THE HAIKU

Finally, here is an exercise that you can use at any stage of the writing process, but which is particularly useful when you are working on draft two. This is when – as we have seen – you want to be clear on the following points: what is the scene, act or play *really* about, *really* saying, *really* doing? What is the heart and essence of it?

The haiku [**hy**-koo] is a form of Japanese verse. It aims to capture the essence of a natural object or a view of nature in one single impression. There are three lines (unrhymed). The first line has five syllables, the second has seven syllables, and the third has five syllables.

Example

Hai	ku	is	sev	en		
teen	syll	ab	les	and	ess	ence
of	what	I	must	say		

Exercise 131

Using the haiku format, give a general impression of your main activity yesterday.

Example 131.1

Took	train	to	mum	but
train	was	late	as	us(e)	u	al
was	there	by	tea	time

Exercise 132

Using the format, give a general impression of how you felt yesterday.

Example 132.1

Ve	ry	an	gry	hot
and	both	ered	wan	ted	to	shout
at	train	man	age	ment

Exercise 133

Take a well-known story and, using the form, give a full impression of its major story-arc.

Example 133.1

Girl	goes	to	Gran	with
grub	meets	wolf	in	trees	he	gets
to	Gran	first	she's	dead

Exercise 134

Take a well-known play and, using the form, give a full impression of its major story-arc.

Example 134.1

Prince	can't	make	up	mind
pre	tends	he's	mad	takes	act	ion
too	late	whole	court	dies

Exercise 135

With the above play, use the form to express what might be the moral or philosophical question at its core: its 'grand theme'.

Example 135.1

If	we	re	fuse	to
Do	what's	right	then	might	we	be
Supp	ort	ing	ev	il?

Exercise 136

With your own play, take a sequence, a scene and then the whole play. Using the form, boil each one down to (a) the essence of its story-action, and (b) the essence of its theme.

9   Performance projects

Much of the work in this book can feed into the creation of large-scale performance projects and devised work: school, college, community, etc. Exercises 11–13 can for example, as we have seen, culminate with the presentation of group-written poems. These could be developed further, with the addition of music, movement, costume, etc. I have seen material from these and other exercises become the basis for some wonderful school assembly presentations, or the basis from which a song-cycle has developed. I recently used some of these exercises with a community group to create the material for a large-scale sung performance piece.

EXERCISES INTO PROJECT

We have seen how some of the single exercises from Chapter 1 can in themselves be the basis for whole large-scale performance, offering (a) a structure and (b) a theme. Here are a few examples of how such exercises can be developed.

Exercise 137 The journey round the circle
Participants: All groups, individual

Look at Exercise 27 in Chapter 1. Use this as a basis for creating a large-group play. Begin with the following structure:

Scene One: Character A + Character B.
Scene Two: Character B + Character C.

Scene Three: Character C + Character D.
And so on until the object returns to Character A.

This is an ideal structure for a process that gives everyone an opportunity to create their own dramatic moment and can be developed in any number of ways:

- In the example in Chapter 1, a pair of scissors was used. Experiment with different objects. Decide upon one that offers the most interesting possibilities, in terms of its own history or properties: a mask, a hat, a book, etc. If it is a mask, what type of mask is it exactly? Where is it from? What does it represent? If a book, what is in it, what does it offer?

- Decide upon the geographical location of the journey the object takes: within your locality, within one country, global, etc. Create a map of the journey on the floor.

- What dramatic possibilities do the different locations offer?

- Develop the characters and the dialogue, using exercises from Chapters 1 and 5. How do the characters change through the action? What effect does the object have on their lives and the choices they make?

- What time frame does the whole story take place in? A day? A week? A year? If there are twelve stories, do we follow them from midday to midnight, for example?

- Experiment with different styles for each scene: comedy, tragedy, thriller, pantomime, etc. Add music, movement and song.

- Each scene has two main characters. Bring in other characters where useful.

- Experiment with having a range of small, intimate scenes and large crowd-scenes.

- Each small scene will have its own theme or issue (see Chapters 3 and 4). List them all. What large theme or issue is suggested by all of them? Could this suggest rewrites, to make this bolder and clearer?

Exercise 138 Further large-scale performance
Participants: All groups

I have already noted the fact that you can use this book as a 'dip-in' resource, as well as a step-by-step guide to creating a play. For those of you wishing to create a large-scale performance, I recommend Exercises 43–53 and 91–93 as ideal holding-forms. The structure of each exercise provides the basis for:

- Individual scenes and characters.
- Interwoven stories and episodes.
- Changing locations and theatrical moods.
- The introduction of music and movement.

Exercise 139 Adapting from the original
Participants: All groups, individual

Stories that already exist can provide a basis and structure for group-devised work. Look at Exercise 130 in Chapter 8.

This exercise explored in a full way the possibilities of re-telling a well-known story in a variety of ways. I first used Little Red Riding Hood in this manner in a summer school for actors. We created a travelling performance, through the grounds and gardens of the building we were working in, taking the audience through the history of Little Red as seen through different eyes: as a revolutionary figure, as a Greek heroine, as a temptress, as a destroyer of wolves, etc. Beyond having great fun playing with different genres, we were exploring how 'the way the story is told' is crucial to how the story is received.

The adaptation of existing stories has a long and honourable history: Shakespeare indeed lifted many of his plots from previous works. As in the exercise, you can divide into groups and re-rewrite a known play or story, in different ways, or from different points of view. All or any of these can become the basis for a scripted performance. Other angles on this method can include:

- What happens next? Take a story and write what becomes of the character(s) after the original ending. What is Red Riding Hood's next adventure?
- Write the scene(s) that do not appear in the story. How did Macbeth and Lady Macbeth meet?
- Get the characters from different stories to meet each other. Red Riding Hood meets the witches from Macbeth!

TWINNING

One method I have used as the basis for drama activity and the development of performance has been that of 'twinning' different groups in a creative process. I have used it in many contexts; it employs much of the work out-lined in this book, and may be of use to those of you involved in leading adventurous, large-scale drama projects.

In 1992, I developed a project with Theatre Centre (a leading producer of professional theatre for young people) to work with two contrasting primary schools. One school was set in the rural flatlands of Norfolk, the other in the centre of Nottingham. The contrast between the backgrounds of the children could not have been more different: all-white and very sheltered from the world; culturally very diverse and exposed to all aspects of modern city life.

The project was called Young Voices, and was led by myself and Theatre Centre's Education Officer, Becky Chapman. The basic aspirations of the project were:

- To create a new piece of work, fully developed with, and finally performed by, the pupils, which would grow from their concerns and imaginations, under the guidance of professional theatre-makers.
- To offer a process through which the two schools would collaborate (at long range) with each other in the construction of a joint narrative.
- To develop thorough working-relations with each school and its staff, and provide a committed input into the life of the school as a whole.

Over a six-month period we worked in both schools for select periods of time, travelling between the two and forwarding the work. The key to the initial exchanges between the schools was many of the exercises in Chapter 1: exercises that enabled these two very different groups of people to get to know each other: Exercises 15, 16, 17, 19 and 22 for example.

In terms of finding a common starting point for a shared narrative, we knew that we wanted something that provided the basis for a strong struc-ture, but wished to keep things as open as possible. We opted for the 'what happens next?' structure: an existing story (one of my own plays, in fact) that concluded in a manner that contained the seeds of a range of possible dramatic avenues.

Much of the work we offered to the groups will be familiar to you now: journeys, the passing of objects from hand to hand (and group to group), mapping territories, creating rich and diverse characters. At all stages of the process the collaborative nature of the twinning was the focus. The nature of the twinning – two contrasting groups – gave rise very naturally to the theme of 'tribes', and thereby to matters of difference, conflict of interests, contrast of customs and history, meetings and outcomes. The outcome of the process entirely reflected the outcome of the play: the meeting of tribes to share their similarities and confront their differences. The collectively created play was presented in each school, with very dif-ferent productions; after which the schools met at an arts centre midway between the two and shared the work. This was the biggest learning moment of all, when two groups who had not yet met, but who had come to know each other through a shared creative process, finally came face to face. Then to see how one story – the story that was theirs – could be told in such a vastly different way.

Since then, I have used the twinning process in many other contexts, nationally and internationally. It is certainly a process through which groups of people from vastly different backgrounds can experience being shared 'citizens of the world', and I recommend it as a unique learning process. It can also be applied on a smaller, more local level: between classes or year-groups, between younger and older groups of citizens. It is one model of how the process of drama, and the event of theatre, can celebrate our differences and nourish what we hold in common.

We have just seen how exercises can become the basis for the creation of material for large-scale work. Each group will arrive at what is at the heart of the performance, in terms of what it is 'about'. By this I mean what the 'issue' (subject matter) and the 'themes' (underlying values) are. These are areas that lie at the heart of all written texts for performance, be it the group-devised play concerning an aspect of community history, or the individual play written for the main stage. Chapters 3 and 4 deal with the distinction between the two.

Appendix A: Adapting the work to the context

When I first started leading writing workshops, I had had no formal training as a teacher, mentor or workshop-leader. All I knew was – through having worked for years as actor, director and playwright – that there were certain useful underlying principles as to 'how stories are made', and that these could be passed on. The problem I saw – which in the end was no problem – was that I was being asked to work in a range of contexts whose participants had varying expectations, backgrounds and life-experiences. Schools and colleges, community-groups, special-needs groups, Lesbian and Gay groups, Black and Asian groups, total newcomers and fledgling professionals; all of whom, I thought, would require totally different approaches and methodologies. I was also rather daunted by the knowledge that, in terms of work in schools, there was a large body of theory regarding 'how children learn', some of which I was slightly aware of, but most of which I was ignorant of.

I stumbled along for a while, feeling an utter fraud, though encouraged by the fact that people seemed to enjoy my presence in the room. I was struggling with 'the problem' – how to put together different sets of work for each different group? Then I had to lead a number of sessions with a variety of groups – ranging from a primary class to an advanced university course – in a very short period of days, with very little preparation time. I found myself presenting each group with the same set of exercises, thinking the game was up. What happened was – and it seems so obvious now, though it didn't then – that I came up with what have been my guiding principles when working with any group:

- Be aware of the general language-experience of the group: what their vocabulary-store is, what their linguistic skills are.

- Be aware of the general life-experience of the group: what their cultural and social horizons are.
- Offer any group exactly the same menu of work, take the first two points into account, adapt accordingly . . . and push the boundaries.

For example, take Exercises 11, 12, 13 and 14 from Chapter 1. Apply the guiding principles to these and they can provide the basis for work in any situation. I have used these exercises in primary schools, with people with English as a second language, on MA Drama courses, with special-needs groups, with Age Concern groups, with technical students at a university in India, on teachers-inset course, etc. From any number of other examples, I have similarly used Exercises 22 and 23 from Chapter 1 in as wide a range of circumstances.

Progressing on to the more detailed work of the following chapters, the same principles still apply. In Chapter 4, you will find that *Little Red Riding Hood* offers the same possibilities for investigating 'what makes a character tick' as does *Macbeth*. Nor have I confined *Red Riding Hood* to any particular age group: she has proved to be as equally useful to MA students as to the primary class. Similarly, primary children have engaged with the scene where 'they plan to murder the boss (or not)', even if they have not yet come to read *Macbeth*. In Chapter 2, the nature of 'theme' and what that means can be investigated in any context, using the same methods, simply by working with texts that are appropriate.

In all of the contexts I have found myself in, I have attempted to offer exactly the same work. On occasions I have had a group consisting of a range of ages and experience. It has been a joy to see that the twelve-year old and the twenty-two year old can both grasp the principle of the Major Turning Point of a story (remember the primary pupil who identified 'The Big Bit'?) and discuss the matter on equal terms. They are both playwrights.

Appendix B: Leading the process

This book is for the individual writer and for groups engaged with creating texts for performance. It is also for people who are leading the writing process, be it the teacher in the class, the workshop leader, the individual writer's mentor, the visiting tutor, the one-to-one dramaturge, or the course leader. The practical exercises in the book are designed to enable all of the above to construct and lead sessions and courses that are appropriate to the context in which they are working. The following notes will, I hope, be of use in specific circumstances.

WORKING WITH THE TEACHER

When it comes to working in a class with teachers, there are a number of things I have come to understand and respect. For those who may be new to this practice, the following points may be useful:

- Teachers are under incredible pressure. There are many that value the input the visiting writer/drama-worker can offer, but even then the welcome presence can be an added burden. Get the teacher on your side, don't just assume they will be there. Find out what they have been doing with the class, why they have an enthusiasm for you being there, and what you can offer that they will be able to continue to feed into their work after you have gone. Always be clear where *your* boundaries are and what you will be offering creatively, but do it in sympathy with the ongoing work of the class.

- Make yourself known and available to the rest of the staff – particularly to the head teacher. Let them know what you are doing. Don't get offended if at first you seem to be regarded with suspicion. As one head teacher, with whom I formed a very good working relationship, after having felt somewhat distrusted, said: 'schools worth their salt don't trust easily; you have to get under their skin'.

- Always be very firm about having another adult from the school in the class with you. That will hopefully be the class teacher, but if they are called away, make sure that it is agreed there will be backup. The teacher will be there to support you, and will hopefully leave you to manage the session without undue interruption; but should any major disciplinary or emotional situation occur, it is not your task to deal with it.

- Pupils are under incredible pressure with the rigours (and terrors) of increasing testing. You are going in as a stranger and – who knows? – you may be another of those governmental types who have come to check up, note down and report back. The work you will be doing may require the pupils to abandon working practices laid down by the needs of the curriculum: 'best writing', spelling and punctuation, etc. If not dealt with properly, this can produce great anxiety. Discuss with the teacher the needs of the creative process, and how the best work is produced if the pupils are not worrying about spelling, handwriting, etc. Make sure that you and the teacher have a united front here, and reassure the pupils that this work is absolutely about not being tested. Constantly remind them of this.

- Always remind the pupils – especially the younger ones – that drawing the character can be as useful as writing about her.

- If there are pupils with English as a second language, always suggest that they can draw upon their first language. Get them to teach those pupils with English as their first language some of their own words and phrases.

- Make yourself available. Let the pupils know a little about you, particularly that you are a writer. I often begin by asking them what they think they might be doing (a) this time next year, (b) in five years, (c) in ten years and (d) how they think they might earn their money after they have finished with education. I then say that I write stories, and that is how I earn my living. This is very important. Some of them will have said that they want to be vets, nurses or airline pilots; others will have invented fabulous lives as pop stars or film stars. You are able to let them know that it is possible to *earn a living* from the thing that you will be doing with them today: making up stories.

WORKING AS A GROUP

Unless we are engaging in a group activity that has clear traditions, strict rules and an enemy (football, the army), we have a bit of a tendency to find collaborative work problematic. That is a generalisation of course, but . . . .

Having observed and led many groups of people who have come together in a creative context, I note that there is a certain urge to push towards the negative and the egotistical when it comes to being in a potentially collaborative relationship. Any group-process or tutor-led workshop must take this tendency on board. So, beyond the task of getting the creative work done, the other (usually unspoken) agenda is 'how to work as a group'. It may be useful to lay down some ground rules, and here are some that I have found useful, particularly when it comes to giving feedback on each other's work:

- Always say 'Yes' to each other's ideas in the first instance. ('I think the scene where the mother's cat dies is brilliant'.)
- When we have given each other confidence by saying 'Yes', we might feel able to offer (and accept) 'Yes, but . . .' ('I think the scene where the mother's cat dies is brilliant, but I would like to know what she felt when her husband died'.)
- When we have established 'Yes' and 'Yes, but . . .', we might find we have enough confidence in ourselves and each other to offer (and accept) 'No'. ('I think it is really not believable or dramatically useful that the cat has the final speech in the play'.)
- Always remind ourselves that reading out our work can be a very nervous-making moment. Listen to each other's work with the attention you would like yours received. I always make a point of saying that – no matter how many years I have been writing plays – the dread moment of the first read through is terrible and a torture.
- When it comes to group feedback on a piece of work, do not allow a free-for-all of 'opinion'. The worst arena for such feedback is when it is thrown open to the floor with a general, 'What do people think about that scene?' Invariably, the negative comes to the fore. Always employ structured feedback.

A METHOD FOR STRUCTURED FEEDBACK

This is a method I and many colleagues use for initial feedback on a new text, be it for the first read through of a new play with professional actors, or a workshop session in a school. It not only allows every voice to be heard, but it avoids unhelpful 'opinion' and opens the door for a range of constructive conversations. It is very simple, very proven and I highly recommend it.

After having read the piece, do not talk about it. Working individually (or in small groups if that is more appropriate), proceed as following. You can use all or any of these, as appropriate to the context and the group:

- Write down a couple of images/pictures that stayed with you.
- Write down three things you liked in the writing.
- Write down three things that interested you in the story.
- Write down three questions about the story.
- As a group, read out each list of things (all the images/pictures first, then all the things that were liked, etc.).
- As the lists are read out, the writer of the piece jots then down. They do not have to respond to them, including the questions. Some of the answers, responses and questions will be similar, some very different. All should be recorded: in many ways, the ones that are similar are the most useful: the same/similar image/question might indicate something crucial about the piece.
- At the end, the writer will have everything down on paper. Here is a sound basis for general discussion (if appropriate) about where they might take the work next.
- Always stress that any of the above is 'free advice/consultation'; to be used/discarded at will. In the end it is the writer's own instinct that will guide them.

REVEAL YOURSELF

I have talked a little about the role of the teacher/mentor/workshop leader and what that has meant to me in my work as a theatre practitioner. What I have not mentioned fully, though have alluded to, is my belief that a crucial aspect of teaching is to include some appropriate level of revealing of yourself to those you are leading.

This is a really difficult one, and I cannot give exercises, examples and outcomes, and you will have to take from this what you will. But I do believe that, if we are going to challenge any group or individual to reveal their souls through a creative practice, we must be prepared to offer something of ourselves to them, in whatever way is appropriate to the circumstance.

'Appropriate' is a key word here. There would be no point in me marching into a primary or secondary school and saying, in a confrontational manner: 'I'm Gay, so there you are', but I will encourage the students to consider and reflect on gender stereotyping in their work, and perphaps drop in an anecdote about my own life . . . where appropriate.

I have talked to black and Asian colleagues who have grappled with the same stuff from the other way around. They march into the situation and – in terms of their race there is nothing to be concealed – they are as equally confined by what they are *perceived* to be as I am by what I am assumed *not* to be. We all, as teachers and leaders, have to deal with the interface of *what we are teaching* and *who we are*.